Farewell, Goodbye, The End?

Farewell, Goodbye, The End?

The Secret History of a Literary Era

BY

CLIFFORD MONTAGUE

Fithian Press
SANTA BARBARA • 1993

Copyright ©1993 by Clifford Montague
All rights reserved
Published in the United States of America

Design and typography by Jim Cook

Published by Fithian Press
Post Office Box 1525
Santa Barbara, California 93102

LIBRARY OF CONGRESS CATALOGING-IN-PUBLICATION DATA
Montague, Clifford, 1907–
    Farewell, goodbye, the end? : the secret history of a literary era / Clifford Montague.
       p. cm.
    Includes index.
    ISBN 1-56474-050-1
    1. English literature—History and criticism—Theory, etc. 2. Literature and history—Great Britain. 3. Autobiographical fiction, English—History and criticism. 4. Characters and characteristics in literature. 5. Autobiography in literature. 6. Livres à clef. I. Title.
PR25.M66   1993
820.9—dc20   92-41747
                                                           CIP

Contents

	PREFACE	7
I	The Progenitors	9
II	The Copy-Cats . . .	22
III	. . . And Mocking Birds	38
IV	The Bitter/Ale Portraits	49
V	The European Seen	58
VI	America's Hey! Days	65
VII	The King of the Beats	85
VIII	No Private Lives	91
IX	The Quicksand Road	115
	INDEX	127

Preface

Roman à clef
Roman—*story*
à clef—*key*
Roman à clef—*key to the story*

FAREWELL, Goodbye, The End? is an investigation of the use of roman à clef in literature from its earliest beginnings, but focusing on this century's prodigious production of such work.

Progressing chronologically by decades, the book shows how its use during this period—the greatest the world has ever known—now has reached the state where its use and abuse has made it almost defunct, owning to the laws of libel and character defamation. Where once the method provided us with unusual "picture books" because of their portraitures, now this method of novel writing is almost anathema to both publisher and writer, and its use today means that such a book must be produced with great timidity or a heavy overcoat of camouflage to avoid unwanted lawsuits.

Besides giving us a history of a branch of literature little known to the world at large, this book brings to life a past method of novel writing that, great as it was, is fast disappearing from our literary scene, seemingly destined to die like the dodo.

Because the use of real people as models for characters in books was once so widespread as to include all classes of humanity—high/low, rich/poor, famous/infamous, lovers/wives, friends/enemies—it would take several volumes just to list all the cases, even if the list was limited only to the most notorious. Hence, this work is restricted to such works as have concerned writers writing about other writers. This restriction seemed the only way to keep a steeple course jumper of a subject-matter within a reasonable corral.

I
The Progenitors

EVERY once in a while there is a prevalent belief that the stream of creative literature is running dry.

It must be admitted that there have been occasions when the state of literature was so low as to induce such a belief. Eventually, however, the periods passed, and the previously low state of literature was seen eventually to be merely one of those transition stages to which all of the arts have been beholden in their course of progression.

At the moment, as in the past, one of the more serious charges thrown at the world of literature—both in the field of drama as well as novel-writing—is that our creators, with their wellsprings of creativity drying up, are turning cannibalistic and feasting off themselves. Except for biography, it happens every time a book, a poem, or a play appears that obviously has one or more of its main characters unmistakenly based on a living person.

The literary world itself, however, is never much shaken by any such revelations. To it, the instance when it occurs is merely the latest example of a certain school of writers who put recognizable people in their books and plays, a school whose members' stock-in-trademark is that they are excessively and strictly factual and who write as though all is fair in literature as in love and war.

Such a school has always existed. The English poet John Milton once declared that artists should endeavor to make works of art of their very lives. The new school, however, has taken his statement and paraphrased it to suit their own needs, and have deliberately written their literary works on the basis of making works of art out of other peoples' lives. Though Richard Brinsley Sheridan once said that no human was ever written down except by himself, some writers in using this method have held veritable Roman holidays in putting their brother authors between covers. (Sheridan himself indulged in the fun. His play *The Critic* savagely lampoons his contemporary playwright, Richard Cumberland, with the name "Fretful Plagiary.")

Although almost as old as the history of literature itself, it is only every now and then that the world is made suddenly aware of a particularly flagrant use of this method of literary character-drawing. The few instances of which the reading world in general is conscious are only a few of the more noted occasions where authors have boldly put their friends and acquaintances (and of course their enemies) bodily into their pages.

While it may be true that in this method of creating literary characters the novelist does not usually draw portraits in photographic style (George Sand, when accused of lampooning a certain abbe, replied that to draw one character of a certain kind one must know a thousand—a statement later echoed by Somerset Maugham), the charge that authors have to a great extent used not only recognizable people for the characters of their books, but have drawn them mostly for the purpose of belittling them, has nearly always existed. It has been voiced since the time of the ancient Greeks up to the present. And just as vehemently as it has been charged, so it has been denied. In fact, it has been so emphatically denied by nearly every writer accused of it that it is a rarity when anyone owns up to it.

The Progenitors

The only well-known case on record where the author acknowledged his culpability was when Charles Dickens admitted that he had "yielded to the temptation of too often making a character speak like his old friend" when he was accused of portraying Leigh Hunt in the character of Harold Skimpole. When Hunt's friends protested further, Dickens went over his book very carefully, and later wrote, regarding subsequent editions, "I think I have made it very much less like . . . I have no right to give Hunt pain. . . ." However, the caricature had gone so far that Hunt was seriously offended. Dickens did his best to remedy the matter, and even wrote voluminously to Hunt: "I am deeply sorry . . . I feel I was wrong in doing it. . . ." But despite his attempts to make amends Hunt never forgave Dickens who, even after the other's death, made a public apology in his work, *All The Year Round*.

In spite of this experience, Dickens on other occasions used people as characters in his books. In *Bleak House,* the character Boythorn is universally recognized as Walter Savage Landor; and when engaged on *David Copperfield,* he wrote to a friend about another friend: "a dreadful thought has just occurred to me—how brilliant he would be in a book!" The truth of the matter, however, is that Dickens' characters are lifted right out of London life, and often right out of his own household. There's a lot of Dickens in *David Copperfield;* his mother and father he immortalized in *The Micawbers*—and his mother a second time in the wife of *Nicholas Nickleby*. Even his wife's sister, Mary Hogarth, was said to be the inspiration for Little Nell in *The Old Curiosity Shop*, while Podsnap in *Our Mutual Friend* was said to be based on Dickens' biographer John Forster. It also has been reported that the Agnes in *David Copperfield* was fashioned after the author's own wife, Kate Hogarth—while his own daughter by Kate (the third) was named Dora for the heroine of *David Copperfield* who was modeled on Maria Beadnell, the author's first love. Dickens, of course, was in turn included in a literary work. Anthony Trollope, in his novel *The Warden,* depicted Dickens as Mr. Popular Sentiment—thus showing him in his role of reforming novelist.

In contrast to Dickens, most authors have been forthright in their denials that they used people in their works. Henry Fielding stated that he never copied individuals, and Steele, in *The Spectator,* expressly denied that he used his contemporaries; he even claimed credit for taking pains to avoid aiming at private persons. However, such authors are in the minority, as a quick glance at many of the world's outstanding authors and their works will show.

The glance will show that Dickens was not the first, any more than he was the last, to put living persons in his literary works. In spite of denials, authors from time immemorial have employed portraiture in their works—some, like Dante in his *Inferno,* enjoyed the sending of their friends and adversaries to hell.

Thus the charge that literature is turning cannibalistic cannot be facilely dismissed. The "cannibalistic" writers—constituting almost a "school" in themselves in the matter of their literary portraiture—outstripped their brother practitioners. Even as the world has always been titillated by the spectacle of portraiture, so has always existed that group of writers who willingly and undisguisedly use their fellow writers as "copy."

Oliver Goldsmith, in his essay on *The Origins of Poetry,* tells how Aristophanes put Socrates on the boards, and even had the actor representing him wear a mask resembling the other's face. Another playwright, Thomas Dekker, depicted Ben Jonson in his work *Satiromastix,* and described his face as "puncht full of holes, like the cover of a warming pan." Jonson, though he professed himself an enemy to the use of personalities, gained revenge by depicting Dekker in his play *Cynthia's Revels.* Then he ridiculed another playwright, Richard Cumberland, in his play *The Case is Altered,* while in *Every Man In His Humor* he attacked another dramatist, John Marston. Not content with this, he undertook the castigation of both Dekker and Marston in his work *The Poetaster*. Even the best-known writer of this time, William Shakespeare, made use of the same technique: in *Love's Labor Lost* he caricatured the dramatists John Lyly, Robert Greene, Thomas Nash, and Anthony Munday. In *Troilus and Cressida* the bard depicted Marston and Jonson. Keeping pace with him in this respect, John Webster and Thomas Dekker, in their work *Northward Hoe,* caricatured George Chapman. All these portrayals in the plays of these dramatists occasioned what is now termed in literary history the "war of the theatre."

Following these writers, and not to be outdone, Alexander Pope used the technique several times: the most outstanding being the unflattering portraits of his erstwhile friend Joseph Addison in his book *Atticus,* his picture of Alpha Behn in the character of Astraea in his book *Imitation of Horace,* and the vile picture he drew of Theobold in his *Dunciad (The Illiad of the Dunces)* which William Congreve claimed held a whole assembly of writers. John Dryden was equally guilty, for he put Shadwell in his work *MacFlecknoe,* and so was Tobias Smollett who caricatured Henry Fielding, in the character of Mr. Spondy, in his work *Peregrine Pickle.* (Smollett, in turn, was depicted in the character of Smelfungus in Laurence Sterne's *A Sentimental Journey Through France and Italy* which shows Smollett to have had a jaundiced eye.)

Others in those early days who were addicted to the practice included John Gay who put Horace Walpole and a whole host of well-known dramatists in *The Beggar's Opera.* In his work *The Life of Dryden,* Samuel Johnson related how bitterly that author resented the ridicule thrown on him as the character of Bates in the Duke of Buckingham's play *The Rehearsal.* In turn, Johnson was mentioned as a likely candidate for the same treatment by the playwright Samuel Foote, who had no scruples whatsoever about the people he included in his works. However, his intention to "take off" Dr. Johnson was abandoned when the Doctor bought a huge stick which he threatened to use. Foote then attacked Richard Sheridan in his play, *A Trip To Calais.* The author Charles Churchill was not so easily put off. In his book *The Ghost* he caricatured Johnson and called him "Pomposa."

Thomas Love Peacock's literary characters were not only ostensibly but almost solely drawn from real persons, and he satirized his fellow authors merely because he disliked their opinions. In one of his works, *Melincourt,* he drew a portrait of Samuel Taylor Coleridge that was not flattering, along with a portrait of Robert Southey, while at the same time he lampooned William Wordsworth mercilessly in the character of Mr. Peter Paypaul Paperstamp. In *Crotchet Castle,* in the character of Mr. Chainmail, he pictured Sir Walter Scott or Horace Walpole (the portrait fits both men) and he again included William Wordsworth as Mr. Wilful Wontsee. In his novel *Nightmare Abbey* he again portrayed Coleridge in the character of Flosky, and insulted him by depicting him as "a man who dreamt with one eye open, which was the eye to his own gain." As though this was not enough for one book, he used Shelley for the character of Saythrop Glowry (who was amused at the portraiture of himself—one of the few men pictured who was not at all disturbed by his representation) while another character in the book who continually spouts paraphrases of *Childe Harold* can be seen as a picture of Lord Byron. He also pictured Thomas Moore.

Byron, perhaps, has the distinction of being the most written-about author of the nineteenth century. With one of the most sarcastic pens of the time, Benjamin Disraeli, long after Byron was dead, portrayed the poet as the character Cadurcis in his work *Venetia,* which also included Shelley as Marmion Herbert and Lady Caroline Lamb, Byron's one-time mistress, as Landy Monteagle. (A lady, however, who wrote of her ill-starred

The Progenitors

love affair with Byron in her own novel *Glenarvon*.)* At the time, the work caused a sensation in the literary as well as the social world of England, but served only to spawn more expository novels about the poet. Chief among these, with Byron as the main character, was Mrs. Humphrey Ward's work, *The Marriage of William Ashe,* Eaton Stanndard Barrett's *Six Weeks at Long's,* Mary Shelley's *Lodore* and again in her book *The Last Man,* Hailie Erminie Rive's *The Castaway,* Frankford Moore's *He Loved But Once,* Lafayette McLaw's *Maid of Athens,* and Maurice Hewlitt's *Bendish.*

Although Disraeli once said that "authors in their books show their own character," he became a writer known for his writing about others. Besides his novel *Venetia* he wrote several more of a like nature—some said with characters "too like." In *Coningsby* Disraeli drew such a vile picture of John Wilson Croker (of *The Quarterly Review* fame), that the other strenuously objected, and in his correspondence and diaries Croker acknowledged that Disraeli more than once had hit home in his portrait of the editor who for once had little recourse but to writhe as he had made other writers writhe under his own

---

*Women writers, even in the early times, were no less prone to use living members of their own sex than the men were. One of the most written about women of the time was Jane Digby (later the wife of Lord Ellenborough) who was portrayed in print even by members of her own family. In 1826 one relative, Marianne Stanhope, published her book, *Almack's* (a three-decker novel of London society) whose heroine was partially based on Jane. In 1830 Lady Charlotte Bury, in her work *The Exclusives,* depicted Jane's outrageously open love affair with a foreign prince. In this work the author showed the heroine as "having been thrown into the midst of the most dangerous class of the most dangerous society in London." In 1837 Lady Marguerite Blessington pilloried Jane in her work *The Two Friends,* of which Edward Bulwer-Lytton who had aided in getting the work published said he thought the book "a very harsh but a very true portrait." The best-known work about Jane, but one of the author's weakest works, was Honoré du Balzac's novel *La Lys dans la Vallée (The Lily of the Valley).* Though the affair was brief—lasting only two months—it promoted Jane to a place in *La Comédie du Humaine.*

scathing pen.* It was this book that ignited the dislike between Disraeli and William Makepeace Thackeray when the latter reviewed it—and reviled it—and even parodied it with a book of his own titled *Codlingsby*. Although Disraeli had previously included a picture of Thackeray in another book (that of Vivida Vis in *Vivian Grey*), his most vicious portrayal appeared in *Endymion*. Here, in the character of St. Barbe, Disraeli called Thackeray "the vainest, most envious, most amusing of men." It was a somewhat ill-natured but accurate picture of Thackeray, who enjoyed a literary reputation equal to Charles Dickens, achieved by depicting high society in contrast to the other's delineation of the lower classes. (*Endymion*, too, contained a picture of Dickens, in the character of Mr. Gushy.)

Of course, after all this, it was only "natural" that Disraeli should have his own portrait done in literature. This occurred when he was pictured in the novel *Robert Orange*, written by John Oliver Hobbes, the pseudonym of Mrs. Pearl Craigie. It was a good "likeness" of Disraeli and it was said that it did him justice—although it was written and published after he was dead.

The "picturing" of Thackeray took place with yet another writer. Charles Lever, in his work *Roland Cashel*, drew a caricature of Thackeray—who was noted for putting living people in his books. It was particularly noticeable in his work *Vanity Fair*, where he was accused of including all of his acquaintances. In

---

*At a time when *Blackwood's Magazine*, *The Atheneum*, and *The Quarterly Review* were riding high in their general condemnation of all writers with whom they disagreed, and damned to perdition, John Wilson Croker (the second editor of *The Quarterly Review*) got his comeuppance. One of the editors famous for giving the low-down in literary reviews, he in turn got what-for. It happened that one of "the victims of his vindictiveness," a woman writer named "Lady Morgan," got revenge for one of his savage reviews of her work. She put him in her next novel, *Florence McCarthy*, as the character Con Crawley. There is no record of a repercussion—but then, even in those days, silence was a potent criticism.

The Progenitors

this book Thackeray drew a vividly vile portrait of John Wilson Croker (in the character of Mr. Wenham, and again as Mr. Rigby in his story "Miss Perkins' Ball" that appeared in his 1857 work, *Christmas Books*). A vicious portrayal was made against his arch-enemy, Edmund Yates, who had lampooned him, and because of whom Thackeray and Dickens quarreled. In his novel *The Virginians* Thackeray gained additional revenge by picturing Yates as Young Grubstreet. Yet another instance of his "portrait paintings" can be seen in his caricature of Bulwer Lytton as "Mr. Bulwig" in his book *Mr. Yellowplushes Ajew*.

But Thackeray was only one of the profuse exponents of putting people in books during the 1800s. Accompanying him in this distinction was Charles Kingsley who, in *Alton Locke*, based the character Saunders Mackaye on his intimate friend Thomas Carlyle—who was also included in *The Warden* by Anthony Trollope whose political novels included almost everyone in the governmental world of England. Trollope included Disraeli as Mr. Beeswax in his work *The Duke's Children*, and as Mr. Daubney in three other books, and as early as 1864 had used Wilfred Blunt in his work *Can You Forgive Her?*

It is well-known, of course, that the original of George Meredith's heroine in his novel *Diana of the Crossways* was Lady Caroline Norton, the poetess and writer of novels of her own in the 1830s, who was involved in a political scandal and accused of selling a state secret obtained from her paramour who was a governmental official. Meredith, as a reader for a publishing house in London, showed some inconsistencies and idiosyncrasies in his work. He was said to have encouraged Thomas Hardy to write novels even though that author did not publish any novel in the last thirty-five years of his life. He also is said to have been responsible for the rejection of Samuel Butler's work *Erewhon*— before that author found another publisher.

Diana of the Crossways was criticized when it came out in 1884 (fifty-five years after the scandal had occurred and seven years after Caroline Norton's death) because it was said to have reopened old wounds—although Dickens had burlesqued the Norton-Melbourne case in his *Pickwick Papers.* When the work first appeared on the scene it raised an instantaneous hubbub, mostly, it is believed now, because of the author's close likeness to the original. (When J.B. Priestley read it a long time later he found the work "baffling and obscure.") While it has been claimed that Meredith used the sensational case because it was still much in the public mind and that might aid in making it a best-selling book, the author had, in fact, used real people in his books before he wrote *Diana of the Crossways.* In his work *The Egoist* he painted a portrait of Leslie Stephen, while in *Rhoda Fleming* he had already portrayed his brother-in-law Edward Peacock Love in the character of Edward Blancove. Meredith's work shows he was not only known to put living people in his books, he seemingly was addicted to the habit. In his work *The Amazing Marriage* (like Henry James in his work *The Portrait of a Lady*) he drew a picture of Robert Louis Stevenson in the character of Glower Woodseer. (Stevenson said "Meredith's veracity is mixed-up with high intellectual humbug.") More yet, Meredith included a portrait of his friend Algernon Swinburne in his novel *Sandra Belloni*—while in his novel *Evan Harrington* he was accused of using many recognizable people as characters. Meredith, as a writer, had found a lode seam of easily worked value—and he extracted as much workable ore as he could without exhausting the seam or working too hard.

One of the most conspicuous examples of this type of literary portrayal concerned the master of *The Gentle Art of Making Enemies,* James MacNeil Whistler. This took place when George DuMaurier, the author of *Trilby,* included a portrait of Whistler in the character of Joe Sibley. The story first made its appearance in the pages of *Harper's Magazine,* running serially between January and June 1894. In the magazine's pages there appeared many illustrations "by the author." DuMaurier had been an art student and, even before the appearance of his magazine serial, had caricatured Whistler in the pages of *Punch*. In the March issue of the Trilby serial, however, the author unveiled his portrait of the painter (Joe Sibley) whom he described as "an idle apprentice, the king of Bohemia, *le roi das truandes,* to whom everything must be forgiven as to Francois Villon, 'a *cause de ses gentillesses.*'" The portraiture continued for several pages, and so there could be no doubt as to his intention the author included two lampooning sketches of the artist. Though the character was a minor one in the story, Whistler made it a point, *à la riposte,* to complain in a furious letter to the editor of the magazine and of course the author, in which he accused DuMaurier of mendacious recollections and poisoned rancor. While his letter of complaint was not as lengthy or as polemic as his usual accusations against his adversaries, it was a typical specimen of Whistler's belligerent letter writing. There were no legal difficulties, however, which is surprising in view of Whistler's fondness for lawsuits. When the book was later published the offending paragraphs had been deleted. The character Joe Sibley had become a personage devoid of any conceit, a good-natured fellow who had never made an enemy in the world. The disguise was complete. The renovated pages were shown to Whistler before publication, and the painter made a great deal of his "victory"—but there were many who saw in the revision more calculated irony than earnest effort to redress a wrong.

Oscar Wilde was also lampooned. It is singular to note in Wilde's writings how rarely his wit or malice was personal in character. He did not direct his shafts against people, but dealt mainly in ideas. However, other writers did not show the same charity, and he was bitterly subjected to the most outrageous ridicule as Reginald Bunthorne in Gilbert and Sullivan's comic opera *Patience*. But some works of this nature have been the making of their authors. Some unknown writers—just as well-known writers—have often used this means to achieve success.

This was especially true of Robert Hichens, whose first book, the 1894 novel *The Green Carnation,* unscrupulously caricatured Oscar Wilde and was the beginning of recognition for Hichens. It has been said that this writer wrote his book to rival E.F. Benson's roman à clef novel *Dodo* but, whether he did or not, he at least created a temporary best-seller. It was also a convenient way for novelists to "get back" at their dislikes or to "even the score" when they felt they had been maligned or misjudged. This was the case involving Henry James who appeared in the story "Lady Tal" (which appeared in book form under the title *Vanitas*) written by Vernon Lee (really Violet Paget) that attacked Henry James (who appears in the character Jervase Marion) because he had given a cool reception to the author's previous 1894 work *Miss Brown.*

The literature of this period is filled with men of letters graphically and vividly described in other writers' books. William Hurrell Mallock, for instance, filled his work with descriptions of many living writers. In his work *The New Republic* he poked fun at Thomas Huxley (as Mr. Storks), Matthew Arnold (as Mr. Luke), John Ruskin (as Mr. Rose), along with Thomas Carlyle and Walter Pater—as the author confessed in his *Memoirs* to using these people. Later, however, Mrs. Humphrey Ward came to the defense of her family (Huxley and Arnold) and in her book *Eleanor* gave Mallock a dose of his own medicine, showing him to be a most disagreeable character. It was at this time, also, that Morley Roberts, in *The Private Life of Henry Maitland,* wrote what is generally accepted to be the private life of George Gissing, even though that author had already pictured himself in his novel *The Private Life of Henry Ryecroft,* as well as in *New Grub Street.* During this time, also, Walter Besant's work *The Monks of Thelema* drew a picture of Walter Pater in the character of Paul Rondelet, while George Grossmith, in *The Diary of a Nobody,* made fair game of Frank Harris—who put many other "lives" under the microscope.

The last decade of the nineteenth century was replete with living portraits in its literature. Arthur Wing Pinero, in his play *Trelawny of the Wells,* pictured his former master in playwriting, Tom Roberson, while George Moore in his first version of *Evelyn Innes* clearly limned William Butler Yeats; in the second version of the novel the portrait was changed to a composite of Yeats and AE—alias George Russell, another light in the Irish literary Renaissance. In turn, George Moore was depicted in G.A. Birmingham's novel *The Seething Pot.* It was at this time that Theodore Watts-Dunton, in *Alwyn,* presented a whole gallery of portraits, among the most notable of which were those of Dante Gabriel Rossetti, William Morris, and J.A. Symonds. Hall Caine also used his literary friends for characters; in *The Prodigal Son* he utilized so many incidents in the life of Rossetti that the book almost may be taken for a biography.

From all the foregoing we can see that the writers who comprised this school of portraying living people in their books have left us a rich heritage indeed in both the literature they created as well as the portraits they drew for us in their books. In fact, it might be said that they have bequeathed us a double heritage: not only did they present the world with a literature that exceeded anything that existed before, they also were the forerunners, forefathers, and progenitors of a school that soon was to expand, multiply, and broaden far beyond what had even been thought possible.

For what the foregoing early writers have bequeathed to us, in fact, is a "school" of writers—and as the progenitors in this matter, as with all progenitors, they were responsible for the "copy-cats" to come after. . . .

II
The Copy-Cats . . .

IF the nineteenth-century writers who used other writers in their books could be called the "progenitors" of the technique, the twentieth-century writers were a worthy group of "copy-cats" who, in many a star-crossed case, either eclipsed or outshone those who had gone before and lighted the way. In fact, it would be hard to say whether the writers who followed the originators were more "copyists" or more "cats"—but the results at least exceeded what the previous generation had produced: the "copy-cats" who existed during the first decade of the twentieth century and continued through the seventies and the eighties have given the world a gallery of portraits—of the living and the dead—that has no counterpart in any other worldwide artistic endeavor.

The books that appeared in England at the end of the nineteenth century were, in reality, just the beginning of a worldwide artistic movement of writers portraying other living writers in books. At any rate, the early books of this nature can be seen as merely something of a cold-front advance of the thunder-and-rainstorms that were to break upon an unsuspecting world. Although no darkened sky foretold this downpour or cloudburst, what actually took place, it seems, was something like a deluge that engulfed the entire world.

The Copy-cats . . .

The most important of this group, in point of popular fame and literary importance, was a writer who bridged the nineteenth and twentieth centuries, George Bernard Shaw. Writing long before the start of the twentieth century, Shaw knew from his drama review days that a literary work would be enlivened by the inclusion of characters modeled on living people. As early as 1907, when he brought out his first dramatic work, *Fanny's First Play,* he caricatured the writer Gilbert Canaan in the character of Gilbert Gunn and included A.B. Walkley and Edward A. Baughan, all three well-known drama critics of the day. While he profusely sprinkled real people throughout his works he did not make too much of a practice of using living writers. (Because he knew they could very easily retaliate?) But in 1917, in *Heartbreak House,* the character of Ariadne Utterworld is patterned on Virginia Woolf.

While Shaw was not above putting living people in his work, it also must be admitted that he was brave enough to include a picture of himself in one of his works, which he did in *Man and Superman.* In one of his early novels, *Byron Cashel's Profession,* Shaw was seemingly prophetic of the literary pretender Gene Tunney by creating him on the printed page about the same time the real-life prizefighter was born. (A later writer who was not so polite was Willard Keefe. In his play *The Celebrity* he made his main character, Barry Regan, not only a prizefighter, but an extreme gentleman and would-be *littérateur,* a character very obviously based on a real person. In addition, author Lionel Britten put the prizefighter in a play by name, but this did not cause any repercussion since the portrait was wholly flattering.)

While Shaw was thus busily using the lives of some of his contemporaries it is only natural that, in return, he should be depicted in other writers' works. One of these was Arnita Lascelles' book *The Sacrificial Goat* that presented a very good likeness of Shaw of the early Shavian novels. He appeared again in Henry James's 1898 novel *The Turning of the Screw* in which, it has been said, he was completely limned, down to the final physical description of the young Shaw that even more pointedly drew him as a political agitator and womanizer. Even earlier than this, in 1894, he was portrayed by his ex-mistress turned authoress, Florence Farr, who painted a complete picture of him as George Travers in her novel *The Dancing Faun*. Later, in 1898, Shaw, in his work *The Philanderer,* depicted her in return. Farr's portrait is accepted as very complete, since she lived with the writer for seven years. When she left him she became the mistress of William Butler Yeats, but there is no record of her having written about *him*.

That was left to Max Beerbohm, whose character Stephen Braxton in his 1919 book *Seven Men* is a picture of Yeats, and Beerbohm admitted drawing it. In turn, in 1920, Beerbohm was used by Ezra Pound in his work *Hugh Selwyn Mauberley* as the character Brennbaum. (In this work George Bernard Shaw also appeared, but as a secondary character only.) The book's main character, Mr. Nixon, was patterned after Arnold Bennett, whom Pound showed to be a Philistine, "a nickel cash-register." While it raked Bennett over the coals, the book raised no smoke and did not burn deeply.

One of the strangest cases of roman à clef occurred early in the modern era, when Louis Wilkinson's novel *The Buffoon* (1916) depicted some well-known characters (as if seen in a mirror) who also helped to write the book. In it such personages as John Cowper Powys (as Jack Walsh), Ezra Pound (as Raoul Root), and H.D. or Hilda Doolittle (as Eunice Dinwiddie) play prominent and forgettable parts. The work became complicated when author Wilkinson included his wife, Frances Gregg, with whom it was shown that Powys was in love, although treated contemptuously by her. Complicating the complications yet further, author Wilkinson reveals that the work was half-written by her—and to whom the writer-husband acknowledges "thanks." A case of mirrors reflecting mirrors, so to speak.

The Copy-cats . . .

It has been believed by many readers that the majority of book-portraits in literature—sketches, caricatures, lampoons, call them what you will—were usually made within a year or two after the prototype had died or that many authors became models for fiction only after their deaths. This was supposedly due to the fear of litigation, since the threat of a libel suit has been known to keep many writers from expounding their spleen, venom, and vindictiveness while their antagonist is alive. But in general the facts are somewhat different. In many cases authors have written of their hates and dislikes while those hates and dislikes were alive. What is surprising, however, is that sometimes it took years after a portrait appeared in a book for that model to answer with a portrait of his own. The perfect example of this is the remark by Sacheverell Sitwell who was devastated by Wyndham Lewis' book *The Apes of God* that appeared in 1930. As long a time as fifty years later (in 1980) Sitwell's response was that it was a "time-bomb of a book."

Again, we can see that it took H.G. Wells some sixteen years before he rebuked, in his 1928 book *The Bulpington of Blup,* the picture of himself in Ford Madox Ford's 1912 work *The New Humpty Dumpty* which had been written under the pseudonym "Daniel Chaucer."

But pseudonyms do not always serve their primary purpose of concealing the identity or true name—of an author or a character. While it has been said that time heals all wounds, there are many outstanding cases in books where the distance of time has seemingly only enlarged or inflamed the wound. One of the most outstanding instances of this was caused by James Joyce's *Ulysses*—a book, it has been said, that was built on the scaffolding of other people's lives, containing as it did many portraits of noted Dubliners (as well as a series of vignettes of the writer Joyce himself).

When *Ulysses* appeared, Joyce's friend, Oliver St. John Gogarty, another Irish writer, fumed because he saw himself in the character of Buck Mulligan which Joyce had drawn. This writer (later Dr. John Gogarty who died in 1957), seeming to realize that he would be remembered as long as the book was read, had a reaction that was almost violent. He called Joyce "that bloody Joyce," and roared, "when I helped him in his youth he has written a book you can read on all of the lavatory walls of Dublin." He wanted to sue but could not because Joyce was in France and not Ireland. Except for the chilliness that developed between the two writers nothing happened until 1939—seventeen years after the appearance of *Ulysses*. Then Gogarty, in his book *Tumbling in the Hay*, included a picture of James Joyce in the character of Charles Kinch. It did nothing to ease the strain between the two writers in their later years. What the world in general does not know about Gogarty the author is that he once crucified another writer, Paddy Kavanagh, in the courts for using him (Gogarty) in the book *The Green Fool*. Also, Gogarty was once successfully sued by another man he had libeled in his (Gogarty's) *Memoirs*. If he had had his way with *Ulysses* it is very probable that he would have ended the existence of the book ... leaving unsaid what he would likely have done to Joyce. Being portrayed was an aggravation that Gogarty was to experience again later in life, when he appeared in yet another book. This was Flann O'Brien's 1964 work *The Dalkey Archive* where he was portrayed as Hackett. That Gogarty did not reply or make a fuss about appearing in this book (as he had on all other occurrences) may be attributable to either his ultimate "surrender" to this novelists' weapon, or possibly he was overcome with a numbness too great to allow any kind of outburst or vociferation.

But these literary droplets were only the first few splatters of the gathering storm to come. As already seen, Ford Madox Ford, when he drew the uncomplimentary picture of H.G. Wells in the character of Herbert Pett in his novel *The New Humpty Dumpty*, started a trend in English letters that soon had many followers. Wells, who was a compassionate man when he wanted to be (although he pictured George Gissing in the character Masterman in his 1905 novel *Kipps,* he was fond of the other author and treated him gently—even going to visit and nurse Gissing who was on his deathbed in France), could also be merciless in his caricatures of the people he portrayed in his books. Besides rebuking Ford in his novel *Bulpington of Blup,* he flayed G.K. Chesterton, an old enemy. Later, he treated Violet Hunt abominably in his novel *Tono Bungay,* and even before these works appeared he had lampooned Mrs. Humphrey Ward in revenge for her attack on him. Also, in his book *Brynhild* (1937), Wells depicted D.H. Lawrence as Alfred Bunter who also had a wife named "Freda." In his book *Boon* (1915), Wells included a picture of Henry James, but that author brushed off the portrait with "I am only—not anyone else—Henry James."

In his book *The World of William Clissold* (1926), Wells presented several people in a more than cursory way—it might almost be called a male memoir of several women, and the author did not hold back in revealing his feelings about the females. Although he had created and run the gamut of scandal in his affair with Amber Reeves, in *The World* Wells seemed to go out of his way to deride and demean—even to caricature as viragos—his affairs with Rebecca West (as Helen) and his eventual *bête noire,* Odette Keun (with whom he had been living for two years) as Clementina Campbell. *The World of William Clissold* is considered today, as it was when it came out, the strangest of Wells' novels, even more so than his autobiography, which is saying a great deal. But Odette got her revenge. After the termination of their affair she published (in 1934) a review of Wells' autobiography; in three stinging articles in a prominent magazine she exposed and detailed her grievances. In this merry-go-round Wells got the last word: he portrayed Odette as the main character in his novel *Apropos Dolores* (1939). The differences that rankled and distraught both writers, to reach the point of internecine disaster, did neither of them any good.

Wells, however, did not escape like treatment. In her work *Pilgrimage* (a series of novels covering the period from 1915 to 1967), author Dorothy Richardson included her former lover Wells in the character of Hypo Wilson. It was something of a literary *tour de force*, since it included not only Wells but his wife, Jane, George Bernard Shaw, the entire Bland family, and of course Richardson herself.

The 1920s saw English fiction writers follow the trend of making public spectacles of private lives; it also saw the expansion of the movement till it became monstrously like a creature whose appetite grows by what it feeds on. What had been a spattering of droplets soon turned into a sudden drenching downpour.

One of the writers of this period who was most accused of peopling his books with characters based on real people was D.H. Lawrence. As early as 1920, in his book *The Lost Girl,* Lawrence drew a portrait of Maurice Magnus in the character of Mr. Day. (Later, his work with the Magnus literary estate was to bring him into conflict with Norman Douglas.) In *Women In Love* he included Katherine Mansfield as Gudrun, and he drew a caricature of Mabel Dodge in his book *The Woman Who Rode Away.* Besides these examples Lawrence included Michael Arlen in his book *Lady Chatterley's Lover* (a small part) but he admitted that the figure of Sir Clifford Chatterley had been inspired by and drawn from the real-life author Sir Osbert Sitwell.

Another writer he included in a book was Norman Douglas, whom he portrayed as James Argyle in his book *Aaron's Rod.* At the time of its appearance Douglas was moved to exclaim only "such tosh I never read." The real disagreement between Douglas and Lawrence started when Lawrence painted a disagreeable portrait of Douglas in the Introduction of Maurice Magnus' *Memories of the Foreign Legion,* which Lawrence published as the executor of the Magnus literary estate. When it came out in print Douglas exploded with such righteous wrath that Rebecca West, in her account of the affair in her book *Ending In Earnest,* claimed that Lawrence had provoked "a savage retort from Douglas that stands high in the dog-fights of literary men."

In his book *Looking Back,* Douglas did indeed accuse Lawrence of putting all his friends and acquaintances in his books willy-nilly—and charged that even such an early work as Lawrence's *Aaron's Rod* had shown his proclivity to use or make "savage portraits." From the fact that Lawrence neither answered nor denied the charge it may be assumed that the denunciation was founded on more than mere fancy—especially in view of the fact that Douglas was not the only member of the writing fraternity whom Lawrence pictured in his work. It was not, however, until 1925 that Douglas, in his book *Experiments,* really became more forthright about the practice than any of the others—accusing Lawrence of deliberately using "the novelist's touch" in biography, stating that such consisted of selecting for literary purposes one or two facets of a man or woman, generally the most spectacular and therefore useful ingredients of their character, disregarding all others. According to Douglas, this technique may deal with facts that may be correct as far as they go, but are too few; and that what an author says may be true but by no means the truth. Douglas stated that this falsifies life, and biography would become a despicable farce if "enlivened or infected" with this pernicious touch. To him, "its use would menace the living, wrong the dead, and degrade a decent literary calling to the level of an old maids' chatter at a tea-party."

That there may be no misgivings that Douglas' tirade against Lawrence was due to the execution of Magnus' literary effects, Douglas was explicit that he was taking issue because of the portrait of himself in Lawrence's Introduction. To end it, he said:

"We shall obviously never have any real manners in literature or society until dueling again becomes popular. Dueling would put an end to these caddish arts . . . there would be no more low-class allusions to living people in books . . . if their authors realized that by next morning they might have half a yard of cold steel in their gizzards."

If nothing else, Douglas' tirade and accusations and protestations against Lawrence's unfair treatment of himself and other friends affords a *plein aire* picture of an author smarting—though with justification—from the spleenful picturization of himself by another author. But many of Lawrence's books caricatured the people he used as models—among them Michael Arlen, Lady Ottoline Morrell, and Bertrand Russell, all of whom had helped Lawrence when he needed help.

In turn, of course, Lawrence was depicted in several other authors' works. One of the first was Kay Boyle's story "The Rest Cure" which later appeared in her book *Thirty Stories*. Again, he was pictured as Richard Ramsden in John Cournos' novel *Miranda Masters*. Along with this he was exposed in several other books, notably those of Mabel Dodge (Luhan), Frieda Lawrence (his wife), and Dorothy Brett. Even though he was "exposed" in these works his career did not seem to suffer except when Richard Aldington published a caustic book that completely debunked Lawrence, a work he entitled *D.H. Lawrence: Portrait of a Genius, But. . . .*

The most notable of all the portraits drawn of Lawrence was that in the character of Mark Rampion in Aldous Huxley's *Point Counterpoint*. Although an intimate of Lawrence during his later years, Huxley had somehow escaped being portrayed by the "impish mortal," as Douglas called Lawrence. The result was that Huxley had no particular axe to grind when he made the picture, and so of course the portrait was almost wholly flattering, a condition to which Lawrence could not take exception, although he did comment wryly that the character was "the most boring in the book, a gas-bag."

But Lawrence was not the only writer represented in *Point Counterpoint*. When Huxley's book came out in England it not only caused a great deal of amusement but for a while afforded

The Copy-cats . . .

the country a popular game—that of identifying the "real" people portrayed in the book.

Huxley was perhaps the most prolific user of this technique of putting living people wholesale, so to speak, in his books. Prophetically, in one of his early critical essays, Huxley had made the philosophical statement that "parodies and caricatures are the most penetrating of criticisms." He made the statement not only as a philosophical creed but almost as a sort of motto by which he produced his books, since all of them contain recognizable personages in their pages.*

In the work of Aldous Huxley, however, the world has almost a lexicon of personalities with which he has peopled his books. While none of his work is parody, *per se,* the people in his work suffered no less—for here can be seen a galaxy of literary stars barely clothed (or disclosed) with fictitious names. The lexicon is a long one, and includes such writers as Wyndham Lewis, Katherine Mansfield, Nancy Cunard, Middleton Murry, and D.H. and Frieda Lawrence, all of whom appear in Huxley's second novel, *Antic Hay,* as well as in other works. While *Antic Hay* came out in 1923, in 1922 Huxley had already showed that he could make good use of the technique; in his story "The Tillotson Banquet" he unmercifully speared Osbert Sitwell in the character of Lord Badgery, calling him "a repellent, stupid ass."

There have been many conjectures why Huxley kept including the same circle of acquaintances in his major books. In *Antic Hay* he pictured Wyndham Lewis in the character of Casimer

---

*The technique of parody has always been a useful, effectual, and even favorite method (or weapon) of literary pranksters and haters. It has existed as a literary device to ridicule or deride, or detract, since the days of the ancient Greeks, as is shown in the "mock battle" of the Frogs and the Mice who poked fun at each other in the *Iliad.* In England the list of literary lions who have had their tales pulled in this fashion would include Evelyn Waugh, Graham Greene, Ian Fleming, James Joyce, and Somerset Maugham.

Lypiatt—but this erratic literary personage was produced, it has been believed by many, because Huxley had lost the contest with Lewis for Nancy Cunard's favors, and Huxley's inclusion of her in the character of Myra Viveash in the same book was his way of showing his displeasure of her choice. There are other instances that invite conjecture. In his book *Point Counterpoint* Huxley not only patterned the character Denis Burlap on John Middleton Murry (under whom Huxley once worked on the *Athenaeum*), he also drew a picture of Katherine Mansfield in the character of Susan Paley, showing her to be exploited, posthumously, by her husband—which so infuriated Murry (the real husband) that he considered challenging Huxley to a duel. Yet Huxley even included one of his relatives: his aunt, Mrs. Humphrey Ward, in the character of Pearl Bellers, in his 1920 book *Limbo*.

Again, in Huxley's books it is possible to see many recurring pictures of people we have previously met in one or another of the novels. In 1921 he pictured in the character Mr. Scogin, in his book *Chrome Yellow,* our old friend Norman Douglas. In 1925 we meet him again, this time as Mr. Cardan, in Huxley's book *Those Barren Leaves*. And the same personage appears for yet another sitting for a portrait in Huxley's book *Brave New World*.

From the fact that Huxley included so many of the same people in almost all his books, it would seem either that he had a deep-seated dislike of the people he ridiculed so much, or that he was incapable of creating any worthwhile character for his books on his own.

For some reason, perhaps because the Huxley picture was not so insulting as the Lawrence portraits, Douglas did not openly disagree with Huxley as he had with Lawrence. Too, as though to balance the scale, Douglas also was accused of using living people in his novel *South Wind,* which was purported to contain an incredible number of recognizable people in its pages.

Keeping company with Huxley in this matter was Compton Mackenzie. (Though he did not write as many novels as Huxley,

The Copy-cats . . .

he put almost as many real persons in his books.) Mackenzie's 1927 novel *Vestal Fires,* was a penned-portrait of Norman Douglas in the character of Duncan Maxwell. It was reported, when the book came out, that Douglas reacted angrily—not because of the portrait of himself—which was favorable—but to the condemning review of it given by Cyril Connolly. (As if to keep the *motif* alive, authoress Olive Manning, in her book *The Rain Forest,* based her character Ambrose Gunner on Cyril Connolly, who appeared yet again, in the character of J.C. Quiggin, in Anthony Powell's *A Dance to the Music of Time.* And, again, as Basil Minto in the Dylan Thomas/John Davenport book *The Death of the King's Canary*.)

When Cyril Connolly appeared (as The Captain) in Nancy Mitford's book *The Blessing* (1951) it was as a small vignette totally unlike the portraits she drew of other people and in other books. (Some said his "small" appearance was due, fittingly, to his importance in literary London.) Nancy Mitford's books, however, usually were portraitures of her family members—especially her four other sisters—to such an extent that they (the books) were referred to as "the Mitford Saga."

Connolly, as we have seen, appeared in other books, but none so deadly to him as Evelyn Waugh's *Unconditional Surrender* (1961) where he appears as Edward Spruance. It was not only an unfavorable picture but one that prophetically proclaimed Connolly's eventual end in the world of literary London despite the earlier acclaims for him. Connolly providentially provided the truth of the prophecy, of course, by his unabating laziness and his vaulting egotism.

Another side of the picture could be seen with the appearance of Mackenzie's 1928 book *Extraordinary Women,* in which the character Hermina de Randan was taken to be a picture of Marguerite Radclyffe Hall, the author of *The Well of Loneliness.* Besides the general public believing this, she did too, and it angered her to the point of despair. But the trend kept on: E.F.

Benson, in his work *Dodo,* fashioned his main character on Margot Tennant, who later became the Countess of Oxford/Asquith—thus showing that no matter how noted was the personage no one was safe from the prying pen of some author.

There were many similar cases, so that it seemed the better known or more important a personage, the greater the risk of being put into a book. The cases to bear this out include Cecil Roberts' book *Scissors,* which mirrored Rupert Brooke as Ronald Stream, whose death cuts short a brilliant poetical career; and Philip Gibbs, who is pictured as Phipps, a war-correspondent, a job Gibbs once had. And, more-or-less in passing, Roberts lambasted the critic J.C. Squires also. Philip Gibbs' writing brother, Anthony Gibbs, once based one of his characters on another writer: in the character of Tony Sutherland, in his novel *Enter The Greek,* he portrayed Michael Arlen.

A number of examples exist: May Sinclair, in her book *The Creators,* used Francis Thompson as the original for one of the many geniuses that throng the book. In her work *Divine Fire,* Ernest Dowson is the prototype for the main character. During this period novelist William Gerhardi, in his book *Pending Heaven,* put his novel-writing friend and one-time collaborator, Hugh Kingsmill, in the character of Max Fisher; in his work *Jazz and Jasper* he pictured Arnold Bennett and Lord Beaverbrook—and apparently had such a permanent grudge against them both that he depicted them again in a second book, *Eve's Apple.*

The writer Hugh Kingsmill, too, had produced his share of real-life people in his books. In his novel *The Will to Love* (written under the pseudonym Hugh Lunn) he pictured the writer Enid Bagnold in the character of Barbara. And he also drew a portrait of Alec Waugh in the character of Glayde in the story "The End of the World" that later appeared in his book *The Dawn's Delay.*

The brothers Waugh, Alec and Evelyn, both novelists of

note, not only appeared in books but drew quite a few portraits of their own in their own books. Alec Waugh was drawn, in the character of Robert Southcott, in A.C. Macdonell's book *England, Their England*. Evelyn Waugh, in his book *Decline and Fall,* drew such an obnoxious portrait of J.C. Squires that it showed he had only contempt for the noted literary critic. In his book *The Unconditional Surrender* he treated Cyril Connolly, as a critic, the same way. Not content only to ridicule the leading literary critics of the time, Evelyn Waugh also, in his book *Vile Bodies,* painted a lampooning picture of Lord Beaverbrook, owner of the *Daily Express,* which at one time was Waugh's employer. But, not content to draw vile pictures only, this Waugh also successfully sued the paper for libel in the criticisms made by the paper's literary critics. But Evelyn Waugh was included in print also. He appears (as Christopher Blow) in Harold Acton's story "A Morning at Upshot's," which later appeared in the book *The Soul's Gymnasium* that served as something of an "answer" to Waugh's forty-year-older picture of Acton (as Anthony Blanche) in *Brideshead Revisited.**

One of the decade's better-known writers was Virginia Woolf, who, if she didn't unlock the door to the private-lives-for-fiction school, at least pushed it farther open with each book she wrote. In her novel *The Waves,* she sketched the literary critic Desmond MacCarthy in the character of Bernard, gently, as compared to her treatment of Edmund Gosse—not because he was a critic or for his critical opinions. She detested him as an individual, calling him a "low-brow and a dowagers' toady." In her 1928 book *Orlando* she drew a mean portrait of him in the character of Sir Nicholas Greene. In a letter to Lytton Strachey

---

*Harold Acton's opinion about putting real people in books is the most unique of all the differing opinions of writers. In his 1948 book *Memoirs of an Aesthète,* he said: "Most people delight in recognizing themselves in a book; it helps to persuade them that they exist." Evelyn Waugh's opinion was that too many writers treated fiction as "a gossip column."

she said, "I know a mean skunk when I see one—or rather, smell one." That Virginia was inclined to use known people to populate her work is verified by her novel *To the Lighthouse,* of which those who knew her family were sure that the Mr. and Mrs. Ramsey of the book were portraits of Sir Leslie and Lady Stephen—her father and mother.* Her book *Orlando* was a biography of Vita Sackville-West, an author in her own right and the wife of the writer Harold Nicolson. But in this instance Woolf had been preceded—by Ronald Firbank, who as early as 1923 portrayed both Virginia Woolf and Vita in his novel *The Flower Beneath the Foot.* Even before this, in 1915, Firbank had shown that he thought himself a superior writer to Rupert Brooke, with his depiction of the poet (before his death) as "winsome Brookes" in his book *Vainglory.* In 1920 Firbank had used Oscar Wilde as the pattern for a character (Lord Orkish) in his work *The Princess Zoubaroff.* The work was almost a biography of Wilde's life as an exile. For all his fiction-biographies, however, Firbank in turn was used only once as a character in a book. Fittingly, this was done by Harold Nicolson (Vita's husband) in his 1927 novel *Some People.* In this work Firbank is the character Lambert Orme.

To the casual observer, or reader, this new form of "realistic" writing had many merry moments when the authors of this "school" exposed and showed certain attributes and traits of character never before realized, imagined, or displayed in print. The general public's opinion of such work was usually one of approbation and approval (as can be seen in the sales records of the books so produced) and the only disquieting thing that seemed to annoy only a few (because it was so far in the background) was that maybe all this "realism," all these disclosures, verged toward something that resembled the cannibalistic. But

---

*Sir Leslie Stephen, who was no small literary light in his own right, had been portrayed also by George Meredith in his novel *The Egoist*—a work that was a mixture of admiration and irony.

the world in general seemed to enjoy this aspect of the new school, and though many of the books written in this period and in this manner might seem to smack too much like tasting only hashed-over tidbits, or only cut-up morsels of a real life, nevertheless there were many who enjoyed the fare where many, many writers were feasting off themselves.

As an era in the history of literature the 1920s was outstanding for a number of things—mainly the number of books its authors produced and the number of romans à clef which appeared. More than any other decade in history, the books of the 'twenties were in the majority only fictional biographies of a lot of other writers. This was the case to such an extent that many of the writers of this era really merited the *nom de plume* "Copy-Cats" . . .

III
. . . and Mocking Birds

THE era that included the two decades of the 1920s and 1930s is very likely the period when personal satire in the works of novelists was at its zenith. It was the greatest period in literary history in which writers inserted themselves (as well as their friends and enemies) in their work—sometimes with a vehement gleefulness and violence the world had not seen since the Augustan age when Alexander Pope brought out his *Dunciad*. In this period the world was treated to such works of distinctive and personal portraiture as D.H. Lawrence's *Women in Love* and *Aaron's Rod* to Aldous Huxley's *Those Barren Leaves* and *Point Counterpoint*; from Wyndham Lewis' *Apes of God* and *The Roaring Queen* to Somerset Maugham's *Cakes and Ale*. While some may say of this era's pictures of living people drawn in books that they are mere pen-and-ink sketches, the truth is that the majority have been portraits painted in oils—generally of the boiling kind.

While Aldous Huxley has the reputation of satirizing his acquaintances in all his books, he was by far outdistanced in this respect by Wyndham Lewis. Of Huxley it may be said that he peppered his works with his contemporaries, the man who surpassed him did so not because of the number of people he used—but for his roasting, boiling, and frying his characters. To many, the colors of the portraits that Lewis drew were seemingly laid on with a palette knife that also had sharp edges.

While Huxley had used Lewis in his 1923 novel *Antic Hay* (Lewis' biographer Jeffrey Meyers states that Huxley wrote the book because of the sexual rivalry between the two men for Nancy Cunard's affections), Lewis did not expose anyone until 1930, when he published his book *Apes of God*. To say that it was a literary bombshell would be an understatement—it was cataclysmic—for the author dared not only to include important people of the literary world, he also said frankly (too frankly for some) what he thought of them.

In this book Lewis' especial dislike was the Sitwell family, and he pilloried them unmercifully, showing them to be "a family of *poseurs,* false and frivolous." He also called them "a trio of clowns." The book so shocked the Sitwells that Edith and Osbert, in separate books, could only reflect how embittered they were by Lewis' shafts. The other member of the family, Sacheverell Sitwell, was so stunned and angered by the book that fifty years later (in 1980) he ranted against the picturizations as "a time-bomb of a book!"

When it came out, *Apes of God* was claimed to be the most vicious satire of modern times, revealing a writer who, in his treatment of human subjects, had a pen with an edge like a razor blade. The reason for this is that, besides the Sitwell family, Lewis painted and shellacked other writers of note—among them his particularly bitter satire of Aldous Huxley in the character of Anthony Hardcastle, along with Stephen Spender as Don Boleyn and Michael Arlen—all three of whom he called "the baser varieties of Marcel Proust." Not content with just this list of notables in this book—in itself a gallery of the exceptionally elite in the literary world—there was one other person whom he was to outline with devastating ridicule again and again to the point where she ranked only a little below the Sitwells. This was Virginia Woolf, whom he pictured in the character of Rhoda Hyman as a precious, snobbish literary fraud. Again, in 1934, he pictured her in his book *Men Without Art;* in 1936 he made more fun of her in his parody of her work with his book *The Roaring Queen;* and he painted yet another caricature of her in his book *Revenge For Love.*

It was only the beginning of a series of books by Lewis that blasted, bombarded, devastated, reviled, and in general volcanically shook-up a great number of people prominent in the literary world. While Lewis could be particular in his criticisms he was seemingly all-inclusive in the number of portraits he wrote down. In his work *Time and the Western Man,* he utilized only thinly disguised pictures of Olive and Vanessa Bell (the art critics of the Bloomsbury Set whom he abominated) and severely criticized Joyce and Pound. In his work *Self-Condemned,* he drew a reprehensible picture of Lytton Strachey, a writer who always mannered his criticisms, more often than not, with unwarranted character references (forgetting that he himself was something of a paragon of unvirtue) but who met his master of innuendo and ridicule in Lewis. During this period it was Richard Aldington who best characterized Lewis' work when he said that he (Lewis) had "sledge-hammered" Alec Waugh's book *The Loom of Youth* in his parody *The Doom of Youth.* In his book *The Roaring Queen,* Lewis' character-drawings included two other writers besides Virginia Woolf. He pictured Rebecca West in the character of Stella Salt, whom he drew as an aggressive feminist opposed to a pompous Samuel Shadbutt who could not be taken for anyone but Arnold Bennett—the *bête noire* of both West and Lewis. In this work, too, he included a portrait of Nancy Cunard in the character of Baby Bucktrout.* In his work

---

*Any literary history of this period would be incomplete if it did not take into account the figure of Nancy Cunard, already mentioned as appearing in several books. She was the granddaughter of the shipping tycoon and reached the apotheosis of her flamboyant notoriety in the second decade of the twentieth century. Before appearing in Lewis' 1936 book, the attention of the world

Paleface, Lewis practically dissected D.H. Lawrence, the man and his work, with the result that forever after there was a hostile barrier between them.

Besides these specific works, Lewis in many instances openly flung barbs and arrows at James Joyce, Ezra Pound, and T.S. Eliot. His criticism was blunt and provocative. When he poked fun at Joyce, the Dubliner responded by attempting, in turn, to satirize Lewis in his work *Finnegan's Wake,* wherein Lewis appeared in the character of Professor Jones. Joyce used parodies, puns, and satires to refute the criticisms he had received. They were, however, feeble efforts in a reprisal unworthy of the giant of *Ulysses.*★

It is only natural, since he had brazenly put his opinions of other writers in his books, that such an active portraitist as Wyndam Lewis was bound to suffer some similar exposure of his own. Overlooking his earlier appearance in *Antic Hay,* Lewis' inclusion in other people's literature was a foregone conclusion, and especially so after the publication of his own book *Apes of*

came in 1922 with her first portrait in Michael Arlen's first novel, *Piracy.* She next appeared in Huxley's 1923 novel *Antic Hay,* then was the model for Iris Storm (Iris March in the U.S. version) of the 1924 novel by Michael Arlen, *The Green Hat.* In 1928 she appeared again, as Lucy Tantamount, in Huxley's *Point Counterpoint* and, also in 1928, was portrayed in the character of Margo Metroland in Evelyn Waugh's *Decline and Fall.* Another portrait was drawn in Richard Aldington's 1932 story, "Nobody's Baby," that later appeared in his book *Soft Answers.* In this work he gave a sour-looking picture of her as a woman of an age older than she had appeared in other books, that of a withered and prematurely aged woman. She died in 1966 at the age of sixty-eight; in 1932 she was thirty-four years old.

★In Lewis' criticisms, however, it is possible to see that he was not trying to hurt his friends but was objecting, in the case of Joyce, Pound, and Eliot, only to their type of work, especially the use of stream-of-consciousness type of writing. In his autobiography, *Blasting and Bombardiering,* Lewis showed his affection for these three in the generous remarks he made about them. Not so strangely, of course, was the fact that this was the only one of Lewis' books that did not give offense.

God. In response to the portrait of herself in that book, Edith Sitwell drew a reprehensible picture of Lewis in the character of Henry Debringham in her novel *I Live Under a Black Sun,* while Osbert Sitwell's book *Those Were the Days* pictured him equally as vile in the character of Stanley Esor. Both books were "answers" to Lewis' caricatures of the Sitwells. Again, in a minor way, Lewis was portrayed in the character of George Heiman in Ford Madox Ford's book *The Marsden Case;* but it bothered no one since its appearance, milieu, and descriptions of the pictures that in the book were to represent Lewis' work had no real concern or connection with the model's actual life or affairs. An equally minor appearance is supposed to have occurred in 1960, when Lawrence Durrell reportedly modeled some of Lewis' personality in the character of Pursewarden in his novel *Clea.*

Perhaps the most important of all the novels in which Wyndham Lewis appeared was *The Golden Falcon* by Henry Williamson. The book omitted few people of either the English or American literary scene, and a brilliant galaxy of writing stars can be seen in its pages: Robert Graves as Manfred; T.E. Lawrence as G.B. Torrance; Siegfried Sassoon as Sheraston Savage; Aldous Huxley as Adolph Stuckley; Arnold Bennett as Enoch Potter; Hugh Walpole as Horace Whipple; J.B. Priestley as F. B. Bradford; John Middleton Murry as Wallingford Christie; Henry Williamson (the author) as James Wilkinson; T.S. Eliot as P.S. Etiol; Wyndham Lewis as Bevan Tarr-Lewis; Gerald Gould as Gerald Gilt; A.A. Milne as B.B. Flynn; Henry Seidel Canby as Harold Vigor Tinby; Ford Madox Ford as Mark Craddocks Speuffer; Stephan Graham as Paul Murray; Isabel Paterson as Isabel Masterson, and Alec Waugh as Alick Peace.

One book in which a character appeared that is at least partly based on Lewis was the famous *Lady Chatterley's Lover* (by D.H. Lawrence) in which he appears as Duncan Forbes. It is well known, of course, that these two writers—Lawrence and Lewis—abominated each other and each other's work. Lawrence claimed that Lewis was too intellectual; Lewis claimed that Lawrence was too emotional or too often guided by his feelings. In this portrait of Lewis, however, the character played such a minor part that today a reader wonders if its unimportance did not reflect Lawrence's dislike of Lewis and therefore was so presented in place of the use of words.

It is interesting to note that Lewis and the Sitwells continued their open dislike to the point of both sides including the other in several books. But even before their particular disclosures in picturing each other in their books, the Sitwells had been well established as characters in other people's books and, of course, putting other people in theirs. As early as 1924 W.J. Turner, in his book *Smaragda's Lover* had pictured the Sitwell family, Edith as Hernia, Osbert as Gob, and Sacheverell as Sago—all three representing the Snodgrass family. Later, Edith was caricatured as Dorothy Merlin in Pamela Hansford Johnson's book *The Unspeakable Shipton*. (The author was warned before publication that some unpleasantness might come from the publication, but she refused to alter anything. Edith was aware of the lampooning, and made snide remarks about it in one of her books, but did not start any suit.) And, as we have seen, Ezra Pound had caricatured Osbert in his book *Hugh Selwyn Mauberley*. Besides this, Robert Nichols in his work *Fisbo* also showed Osbert as a hypocritical character. From these occurrences it can be seen that Osbert Sitwell was the main focus of the "exposé" of the Sitwells. But in his turn Osbert proved to be no slouch in getting other people into his books—both before as well as after he had been "exposed" by others. In his 1924 story "Friendship's Due"—which later appeared in his book *Triple Fugue*—he drew a caustic lampoon of Ferdinand McCullock in the character of Lomis McQuilland, shredding his reputation because the other writer derided the poetry of the Sitwells by calling it "the Asylum School of poetry." In the same book he took pot shots at the poet, essayist, and critic Edmund Gosse, and depicted him as a despicable character. Osbert also got adequate revenge against Aldous Huxley by including him in his story "The Machine Breaks Down," and later, in 1938, at last got his revenge against Ezra Pound by putting him in his book *Those Were the Days*—as the character Manfred Moberley, a take-off on Pound's main character in his book.

Osbert Sitwell was often reckless in his portraits and his language in his books, but his writing career was scarcely to be affected or blighted—even though he once had to pay the equivalent of $1250 to settle a libel suit arising from his book *Dumb Animals and Other Stories*. Besides the monetary cost the book had to be withdrawn from publication in England.

Edith Sitwell, for her part, was no less an iconoclast of reputations. As we have seen, she included Wyndham Lewis in the character of Henry Debringham in her work *I Live Under a Black Sun*, but it was very clear to all readers of her book that her only purpose in creating the character was to attack him—since the character performed no function in the book. And when, in her autobiography, *Taken Care Of*, she took a spleenful delight in telling embarrassing incidents about Lewis that stressed his poverty, Lewis, in turn when he learned of her plagiarizing the work of several contemporary poets, strove to publicize her peccadilloes to the whole world. The Lewis-Sitwells' affair has no counterpart in any other literature. It was as if, in their books, all the writers were trying to present us with a family picture—a sort of family album—with each one showing us the other side of the "other" family.

The decade of the 'thirties continued the same pattern as had been set by the writers before. When Richard Aldington said that Wyndham Lewis had "sledgehammered" Alec Waugh, his remark only brought to mind that, in his criticisms and portrayals of living people in his books, Aldington could rank among the best in this school of writers. He was characteristically sour and ill-tempered about many people—mostly writers—and he frequently turned against even his friends, including D.H. Lawrence, Ford Madox Ford, Norman Douglas, and T.E. Lawrence. In his book *Death of a Hero* (in which he caricatured T.S. Eliot in the character of Waldo Tubbe as an American passing himself off as an Englishman, and Wyndham Lewis as Frank Upjohn, a painter who starts a new "school" as soon as the previous one proves disastrous) the main target was T.E. Lawrence, the author of *Seven Pillars of Wisdom*. In this work he debunked this mysterious Lawrence with pen-pricks of acid. And when he was informed that some of D.H. Lawrence's character Sir Clifford Chatterley in *Lady Chatterley's Lover* was partly based on him, Aldington responded not with a sledgehammer but a cleaver. In his book *A Portrait of D.H. Lawrence: A Genius But...* he dissected this Lawrence to the extent that one critic said the book "dripped with malevolence."

As the decade grew older so its addiction to portrayals grew, so that it seemingly was a period when hates and dislikes ran hot and high and consideration for others' feelings, or even common sense ethics, ran cold and low. It was a contagious fever that seemed to run rampant in the writing fraternity. It infected even the detective-novel genre. In his 1933 work *Hag's Nook* the mystery writer John Dickson Carr used Gilbert Keith Chesterton as the model for the character Dr. Gideon Fell—and continued to do so for a series of books. In 1971, in his novel *The Naïve and Sentimental Love,* John Le Carré pictured another novelist, James Kennaway, with whose wife Le Carré had an affair (primarily engineered by Kennaway himself because he "wanted something to write about")—but it was she who exposed it to the world in her book *The Kennaway Papers* whose theme showed it as the cause of his suicide. In 1975 biographer Janet Hinchman, in her book *Such a Strange Lady* deliberately limned the mystery writer Dorothy Sayers who had, in 1935, portrayed novelist Doreen Wallace (as Catherine Benedick) in her novel *Gaudy Night*.

But other writers continued the use of living people. Roy

Campbell, in his 1933 work *Georgiad,* caricatured Vita Sackville-West and her husband Harold Nicolson as the characters Georgiana and Mr. Georgiana. Also, authoress Angela Thirkell, in her books *High Rising* and *Demon in the House,* included a picture of a fellow writer, E.V. Lucas (in the character of George Knox) who had helped her get started in writing. (Lucas had already appeared in print before this, in the character of Peter Davies in the book *Peter Homunculus* by Gilbert Canaan.) Along with this listing there would also be Malcolm Muggeridge's character Flavel in his book *In a Valley of This Restless Mind,* published in 1938, which was based on the poet, novelist, and literary critic Gerald Bullett—but the use of a model was admitted by the author only when the book was republished in 1978. Following this course of novel writing was Christopher Isherwood who put his friend and fellow writer Edward Upward in two of his books: as Allan Chalmers in the 1928 work *All the Conspirators,* and the 1938 book *Lions and Shadows.*

During the first half of the 1940s the world was engaged in a war that preempted all other activities, including the work done in most of the arts. Only in the last half of this decade was literature "free" enough to employ in its own somewhat private preserve, or territory, its pursuit of using living persons as models for fiction, or, more explicitly, using writers. It was as though our authors, like a candle whose flame flutters in a draft, wavered in the practice that during the 'thirties had reached its zenith in the new-found "realism." It was not until near the end of the decade that it again appeared in any literary work. It was not because the mother-lode had run out; rather, it was the danger in this kind of work that caused its sharp decrease and near cessation. This was the advent and increasing use of lawsuits and threats of lawsuits that brought the decided lull in the practice.

A lull, but not a total cessation, for in 1949 one of the earliest of the books to use a living model—and of course a writer—was Stevie Smith's book *The Holiday,* which pictured George

Orwell not only once but twice. Not only did he appear as Basil Tait in the book but also as a second character as well. Smith explained by saying, "Splitting George in two seemed to lessen the risk of libel."

Another writer who used the method was Henry Williamson who in 1964, in his book *The Power and the Dead,* drew a cruel portrait of John Galsworthy in the character of Thomas Morland—showing him to be a worn-out and declining author of popular but insignificant fiction. Again, in 1965, he portrayed Michael Arlen as Dikran Michaelis in his book *Phoenix Generation.* And of course, Williamson was portrayed in turn; in the character of Stephen Taylor in Frederic Raphael's 1976 novel *Glittering Prizes,* he is shown as a man who, in spite of being a Hitler-phile and a man of appalling ideas, he was not himself an appalling or untalented man. It was a long way from the picture that had been painted of Williamson and his wife, in the characters of Mr. and Mrs. Brian Stucley, in S.P.B. Mais' 1928 novel *Orange Street.*

The faltering technique made its appearance in a few works of some of the die-hard authors: i.e., the old-fashioned writers. In 1974 novelist C.P. Snow depicted novelist William Gerhardi, in the character of Julian Underwood, in his book *In Their Wisdom.* The writer Cyril Connolly appeared in two books—in Harold Acton's story "The Morning at Upshot's" (which later appeared in the book *The Soul's Gymnasium*) and Anthony Powell's *A Dance to the Music of Time.* In the first he is pictured in the character of Cecil Cuthbertson; in the second he was pictured as the character J.C. Quiggin. Also, in 1983, Clive James' book *Brilliant Creatures* contained the portraits of Tom Stoppard and his wife, the writer Miriam Stoppard, in the characters of Tim and Naomi Strippling.

Perhaps the most startling of all the books written in the last half-century was the one published by Anthony West, the son of Rebecca West and H.G. Wells, *The Heritage.* Not only did the work contain the outright character drawing that was so popular in the 'twenties and 'thirties, this 1955 roman à clef was an outright attack—of a son against his mother.

In his portrait of the character Naomi Savage, West tried to show Rebecca West as a selfish and mendacious writer who had attempted to hurt him as much as she could. He accused her of hostility, aggression, and spitefulness—forgetting that he was guilty of the same things. In 1984 Rebecca West's biographer warned the public that Anthony was trying to destroy the personal and professional reputation of his mother, who was the more distinguished writer. In his book Anthony West included a portrait of his father in the character of Max Town, and showed his approval and support of him and his work while degrading that of his mother. In England Rebecca West was able to halt the distribution of *The Heritage* until her death. What she had not been able to stop was her son's use, against her, of a pen as sharp as a dagger.

It was a sad picture of two members of a gifted family at sword's point with each other.

IV
The Bitter/Ale Portraits*

THE showers of books by writers depicting other writers that appeared on the literary horizon in the 1920s and 1930s were, as we have seen, in the nature of a good solid rain. In the affair concerning *Cakes and Ale* and later *Gin and Bitters,* the storm that resulted from these two books was more than just an ordinary storm—it was a deluge that seemed about to engulf everybody in the literary world with such a drenching that all concerned (and many who were not) were made miserable and unhappy. In fact, it was a storm that stood singularly alone—and still does even more than half a century later—because it had no rivals or counterparts in twentieth-century literature. It was a cause of such flooding of book reviews, newspaper, and magazine articles that half the literary world found itself awash in a turbulent swirl of waters while the other half seemed to be trying to flounder to a shore. It was more than a deluge. Where the Biblical flood had lasted forty days and forty nights, this storm lasted twenty years.

*Ale is reputed to be one of the best drinks in England—a draught that refreshes and resuscitates when one is wearied. Bitters are used to give a tart taste to drinks that generally would be mild to the point of being bland. In Somerset Maugham's *Cakes and Ale* and Elinor Mordaunt's *Gin and Bitters* we have two perfect examples, even in literature, that some drinks do not mix.

Maugham's book came out in late 1931 and almost at once created controversy that caused other controversies. It had an immediate *succès de scandale* that ranked it only with the famous James Whistler suit against John Ruskin.

As a novel, *Cakes and Ale* was slight, with little plot, but it contained a brilliantly and ironically pictured gallery of portraits, as well as some malicious commentary on the English literary world ranging from the 1890s to the 1920s. Also, it contained some acute and iconoclastic literary criticism; and this, coupled with the author's usual acidulous habit of taking occasional savage swipes at contemporary authors or habits of mind and taste, brought it immediately to the attention of the writing world. As one critic remembered, the author supposedly was not satisfied to satirize only one character but filled his work with pointed remarks about many allegedly recognizable contemporary authors, and in dealing with these characters he had made full use of double-barbed irony and cynicism.

Not only was it claimed that he satirized Thomas Hardy in the character of Edward Driffield, and the second Mrs. Hardy in the character of Driffield's second wife—but it was claimed that Maugham had maligned many living writers and, in the portrait of Alroy Kear, poked sarcastic ridicule at another contemporary and distinguished figure and writer, Hugh Walpole. The critics also pointed out that Maugham had painted with unpleasant hues additional portraits of the literary figures of his era. It was noted that the lion-hunting social hostess Mrs. Barton Trafford in the book was a thinly disguised exposure of Mrs. Sidney Colvin, while the novel's poet Jasper Gibbons, sponsored by Mrs. Trafford and then dropped when his value as a coming poet disappeared, was claimed to have been a picture of Stephen Phillips, although John Drinkwater considered the figure to be a cruel caricature of himself. Here also could be seen the critic Edmund Gosse (as Algood Newton), with passing references to Proust, Carlyle, Meredith, Pater, Mrs. Humphrey Ward, Ouida,

Henry James, Lytton Strachey, E.M. Forster, Evelyn Waugh, and Compton Mackenzie. The book swarmed with vignettes of real writers, most of them satirized unmercifully (none shown in a favorable light)—except, surprisingly, the tender treatment given Driffield whom everyone took to be Thomas Hardy and believed Maugham had maligned.

To say that *Cakes and Ale* created a furor would be an understatement. At the very least there was much discussion about the book—by the public as well as in literary and publishing circles—and there soon grew two camps of believers, each ready to do fistic battle, literally and figuratively, over the book. For the general public, however much it enjoyed the authorial uproar, there were some serious questions. Why had Maugham written the book? Was its purpose to malign or satirize only? To many it seemed that the author had surely overstepped the bounds of decency since not only one person was supposedly maligned but a good many people, and not only individuals who were living but some dead ones as well. Was it true, as some who did not need to read between the lines seemed to know, that the novel's justification might be a malicious and deliberate attack and not just an impersonal and disinterested spoof of insightful mockery?

These questions and the critics' ragings about both Maugham and his book soon became distinguished by the fact that the hullabaloo merely brought more outbursts in print, some of which brought out facts about other works by Maugham.

In the past, and for a great part of his career, Maugham had built for himself a widely known reputation for creating book-characters from living people. In his first novel, *Liza of Lambeth*, he shockingly revealed a certain class of Londoners. The work was attacked from the pulpit, but it brought the unknown writer to the attention of the public and the publishing world. In his novel *Of Human Bondage*, a partially autobiographical work, he portrayed not only himself but also Violet Hunt in the character of Norah Nesbit. Again, in his novel *The Moon and Sixpence* his main character was drawn with a resemblance to Paul Gauguin, the French artist. Because for much of his career he had used recognizable models for his characters, and had been accused of the practice many times in his novels and short stories, Maugham once felt compelled to publish a disclaimer, and in his book of short stories *First Person Singular* there appears an introduction explaining his method of character drawing. But, in spite of his "explanation," few had ever forgotten that the first edition of his book *The Painted Veil* excited much attention and comment in Hong Kong because the name of the city in the book pin-pointed the officials derided. It caused so much of a stir that the publishers deleted the name from subsequent editions. They did so from one page but forgot that it appeared on another.

Thus, when *Cakes and Ale* came out it did not take the critics very long to discover and point out the likenesses of Maugham's characters to certain living writers and also a dead one.* In England, the book received violent reviews and savage attacks, including one by J.B. Priestley who suggested that a retaliatory book be written about Maugham. The original criticism about *Cakes and Ale* centered on the character of Driffield whom many took to be copied after Thomas Hardy, but this was temporarily checked when Maugham declared that he had not copied from Hardy at all, and his character might as well have been based on George Meredith. Then it was pointed out that his fictional Driffield was supposed to have had a book banned, and Hardy, too, had had a book banned but Meredith had not. The critics in addition cast about for another reason, and they found one easily enough. From the savagery of their new attack and the denunciation they used in disclosing their discovery, it

---

*Foremost among the finger-pointers in the United States were Mark Van Doren in *The Nation*, Howard Coxe in *The New Republic*, and Stanley Went in *The Saturday Review of Literature*.

must be remarkable to a reader, today, how they overlooked it in the first place—since it had been put before everyone in the very first chapter. This was Maugham's portrait of the character Alroy Kear. He was not bombastic, malicious, mean, or vindictive; it was, on the contrary, nothing but a loud damning with nothing but praise.

Barely two months after the appearance of Maugham's *Cakes and Ale* there appeared on the literary scene another book, *Gin and Bitters,* which was a reply to Maugham's book. This work was published under the pseudonym of "A. Riposte" to conceal the identity of the author. As a novel it was scarcely original because it was an obvious attack on a man who had written a novel and its subject-matter was thus more or less dictated by what had gone on before. Also, on reading the book, and rereading J.B. Priestley's review of *Cakes and Ale,* it can be seen that that author's suggestion that a novel based on Maugham was picked up and acted upon by the author of *Gin and Bitters,* with the result that the work appeared to be not a novel in the true sense but simply a vicious and savage attack on another writer. Though "A. Riposte" (which is a cleverly returned thrust in fencing) was used by the author, the work was more in the order of an insensate slashing.

Gin and Bitters was a bitter book, and a recklessly indignant one. There was not much to distinguish it in the United States except the hullabaloo raised by the critics, and the oddity of its anonymity. Of course, when it first came out there was a great deal of speculation about the identity of its author, but the publishers refused to reveal the real name in order to whet public curiosity and increase sales. As a result many people conjectured that the work had been written by Walpole as a defense, but some claimed that the writing could not be identified as his and was probably written by one of his admirers. Nevertheless, in a short time after its appearance, the publishers divulged that the writer was a woman. However, since *Gin and Bitters* did not have a long life—all interest in the work soon became lost—the author's real name at last came to light. "A. Riposte" was Elinor Mordaunt, the pseudonym of Evelyn May Clowes, noted for her travel writings and articles in women's magazines.

When her book was published in England, under the title of *Full Circle,* and her name appeared on the title page, there was even greater furor than was occasioned in the United States. One of the differences between the two editions was that the English version omitted the foreword, to the effect that none of the characters represented any living person, and for this reason an action for libel was promptly threatened by Maugham, who also sought to restrain the publication of further copies. Because of the threatened suit the volume was withdrawn from sale in England and the issue did not go to trial.

What is remarkable in the case of these two books—both biting, scathing, and even malicious satires though they were—is that they created a great deal of discussion, examination, re-examination, and denunciation (from the first day of their publication) such as no other piece(s) of literature had undergone for two centuries . . . and they continued to remain in the limelight for almost twenty years. It might be said of each of them, each in its own way, was the zenith and nadir of its kind, and both the worst and best of its kind.*

The affair of *Cakes and Ale* and *Gin and Bitters* did not—by a long shot—lessen any of the proclivities of writers to use other writers as characters in their books. And of course Maugham was used, much as he used people, as a model for a character, and so appeared in several notable books. One of the first was

---

*It is interesting to note what Hugh Walpole had to say about *Cakes and Ale.* Writing on "The Tendencies of the English Novel" in the *Fortnightly Review* two years after the book's appearance, he said: "Somerset Maugham has published an amusing and witty novel in *Cakes and Ale,* and some admirable short stories; but he has never approached the size and dignity of *Of Human Bondage.*"

the work by his novelist friend Ada Leverson, whom Wyndham Lewis had used for his character "Sib" in his work *The Apes of God*. In her 1911 book *The Limit* she gave Maugham the name of "Gilbert Hereford Vaughan, known mostly as 'Gillie.'" Another was playwright S.N. Behrman, who in a stage adaptation of one of Maugham's stories, *Jane,* included Maugham in the character of Willie Tower and used much of Maugham's background and propensities—but it was notable only for the fact that the work did not create a stir of any kind. Noel Coward also wrote much about Maugham, both in his sketches and novels and in one play. In the earliest, his 1935 *Point Valaine,* he pictured him and dedicated the work to Maugham in order, so it was said, to reduce the chance of a sharp retort or reprisal. In his 1956 novel *South Sea Bubble,* he again portrayed Maugham in the character of John Blair-Kennedy; in *A Song At Twilight,* his 1966 play (one year after Maugham's death), he based his main character on Maugham in the role of Sir Hugo Latymer. (It has been said, by one critic reminiscing about Maugham, that if Coward had written biography instead of sketches he would have provided some noteworthy observations about Maugham.) In addition, even after he was long dead (1980), Anthony Burgess, in his novel *Earthly Powers,* used Maugham as the prototype for the character Kenneth Marchal Toomey. Of course, the greatest picture of Maugham is in his own epic novel *Of Human Bondage,* where he presented himself in the character of Philip Carey.

There are many interesting sidelights in this affair, even though it may take many years to come to light as, in this case, some twenty years. In the hubbub over *Cakes and Ale* Maugham was severely criticized for using actual people as characters in his books—but it was also true that he was not the only writer in this case to use the method, since Walpole also used the technique and was himself guilty of putting a living writer in one of his books. In his work *Fortitude,* the character Mrs. Launce is an accurate portrait of Mrs. Marie Belloc-Lowndes, the wife of Hillaire Belloc. In the same book he included a portrait of Henry James in the character Henry Galleon; it was a pleasant picture because James had helped Walpole in his literary career. (In fact, James had earlier pictured Walpole, as Hugh Quibble, in his 1911 book *The Outcry*. Walpole is reported to have said of it: "The physical description is like, the rest not at all.") In addition, Walpole is reported to have included other living people in his book *Harmer John*.

While Maugham was the *bête noir* of *Gin and Bitters,* Hugh Walpole was also included in the book, as Mr. Polehue, and though it was an innocuous portrait he did not get off so lightly in another work that came closely behind. This was *Cold Comfort Farm* (1932) in which the author, Stella Gibbons, poked sarcastic fun at Walpole (in the character of Anthony Pookworthy) for his actions in heralding new writers as less than altruistic. (Somerset Maugham said much the same thing: when Walpole lectured on younger writers there was always a run on Walpole's books but never a run on the authors he talked about.) Stella Gibbons derided Walpole even further. She adorned the name of Anthony Pookworthy with the letters ABS and LLR— Absolute Back-Scatcher and Licensed Log Roller.

What might be called the icing on the cake, however, occurred when Walpole, made wretched because of his portrait by Maugham, in 1937 (six years after the appearance of *Cakes and Ale*) in turn portrayed Maugham, in the character of Archie Bertrand, in his novel *John Cornelius: His Life and Adventures*. The work was not malicious or particularly detracting, and mostly because Maugham was not specifically targeted, the public did not learn much about it, and the work died a quick and quiet death. It was a sad swan song of a man who once had trod the slopes of Parnassus.

Cakes and Ale dramatically affected Walpole's reputation as a writer and embittered the last years of his life. He accepted (whether with doubts or misgivings is unknown) Maugham's assurance that he was not the original for the portrait of Alroy Kear, and so remained on friendly terms with Maugham—even going to the extreme of attacking the writer of *Gin and Bitters*. This amused many literary friends for, though Walpole accepted Maugham's statement that he did not have him in mind, no one else really did. The final result of the *Cakes and Ale/Gin and Bitters* portraits is that the book by Maugham was the ruination of Walpole, ending both his literary career and reputation. Although by 1931 he had already written thirty books, the stigma of the figure of Alroy Kear—so said Anthony West—"extinguished Walpole as a serious literary figure."

It was not until after Walpole's death in 1950—twenty years after his book came out—that Maugham, in an introduction to a new edition of *Cakes and Ale,* admitted that he had, indeed, intentionally used Walpole for the character of Kear—and to support his use he pointed to the biography of Walpole by Rupert Hart-Davis that showed he was justified in showing Walpole as "being an awful person."

When *Cakes and Ale* first came out Walpole was reported to have tried to laugh off the ridicule with the statement: "I shan't forgive Willie easily. The beggar has drunk my claret."

The reference was a most apposite one, showing that claret was another drink that did not mix well.

V
The European Seen

JUST as much as in England, the writers of Europe have created a literary scene that is also, at once, an authorial "seen" as well. Here, too, the writers have exercised not only their powers of observation and invention, but also their inclinations, opinions, and beliefs, all set down in inerasable ink, of what they knew—or if they did not know, thought—of their brother writers.

Here, too, the use of the living writers as models for characters (if not the complete and outright use of those writers' characters and lives in books) was employed just as extensively. Nor can it be said that the foreign writers so treated fared any better than any other writers elsewhere. In France, particularly, the practice always had wide vogue, even in the earliest days, as we can see in Palissot's play *Philosophers* that ridiculed Helvetius, Rousseau, Voltaire, Diderot, and others; the drama caused Voltaire to take such umbrage that he replied with another play in which the character of Palissot was ridiculed in turn. Also, it is now well known that the allegories of Voltaire are not simply allegories, but are stories of real people.

Molière was likewise plagued, and plaguing. In 1663, one of his works was believed by the dramatist Edme Boursalt to be a caricature of himself, and so he in turn ridiculed Molière in his work *Portrait of a Painter*—which Molière, of course, had reason to believe was a caricature of *him,* and so answered it with an avowed denunciation of the other writer. All this, taking place in 1663, shows that authors even then were not slow to use their fellow writers while at the same time ridiculing them.

In additon, Théophile Gautier is the authority for the report that Rabelais, in *Panurge,* made fictional capital of the life of François Villon, while Balzac, of course, is well known for the use he made of his acquaintances, especially his literary friends, in his work. It was not only his acquaintances that he used, but sometimes his competitors or rivals in the field of literature. This is noticeable in his work *Lost Illusions* where he sketched the character of Lucien de Rubempre from Alberic Second, a young Parisian writer, while in the same book he revenged himself against the critic Armand Carrel by depicting him as the character Michael Chrestian. In his work *Modeste Mignon* the character of the poet Canalis in the story is based on the poet Lamartine. Balzac, who was a prolific womanizer as well as a novelist, in his work *La Duchesse de Langeais,* revenged himself by boldly ridiculing the real-life Marquise de Castries, who was the model for La Duchesse just because she had been repulsed by the author's appearance, of which he was generally careless. The work and the revenge did nothing to aid the author's career. He then wrote of his love affair with Jane Digby in *Le Lys dans la Vallée.* Seemingly Balzac was as unstoppable in using people as models for his characters as he was unstoppable in writing about his love affairs. (This the author himself admitted in one of his letters: "the total of the women who have had the impertinence to recognize themselves . . . stands at seventy-two.")

But there was one woman whom Balzac wrote about more than once. This was George Sand. She appeared first as Julie de Aiglemont in Balzac's 1831 novel *La Femme de Trente Ans.* (In this work Balzac had the perfect example of character drawing as seen in Stendhal's epic work *The Red and the Black,* where the countess Clementine de Curial served as the model for the book's Katherine de la Mole.) Here, too, Balzac included a picture of Jules Sandeau, Sand's lover at the time, who had also been Balzac's secretary some time before. Then she appeared as the character Félicité des Touches in his work *Lost Illusions;* next as the title character in his book *Honorine,* and last as Camille Maupin in his 1844 book *Beatrix,* wherein he portrayed the world of Sand and her coterie of friends and acquaintances.

Sand, in her lifetime, may be said to have been the most-written-about writer of her century. For long before Balzac portrayed her she was depicted by Jules Sandeau in the character of Marianna in the novel *Marianna Belnave,* and of course she answered with a picture of him in the character of Horace Dumontet in her book *Horace.* (It is suspected that she also included a picture of him in the character of Stenio in her early book *Lelia,* which caused a sensation when the critic Gustave Planche fought a duel in defense of her literary honor against a critic who had attacked the book. It has been said that, although the shots misfired, the sales of *Lelia* shot up.) Her affair with Alfred de Musset is galleried in his book *Deux nuits d'excès* where she is the character Comtesse Gamiaui. He pictured her again, in the character of Brigitte Pierson, in his book *Confessions of a Child of the Age.*

While it is true that Sand often kissed and told in her books she also, like Balzac, was not averse to putting herself under the spotlight for examination—with the result that in her sketches and images, as well as full-length character drawing, we have portraits that provide a veritable gallery modeled from real personages. In her novel *Lucrezi Floriani* she depicted herself as the heroine and her lover-hero, Benjamin Constant, as Lebensei. (In retaliation, he evened the score by writing his side of the affair in his book *Adolphe* in which, of course, Sand came off second best.)

One of the outstanding literary affairs attributable to Sand, and one that remains in the consciousness of the literary world of today, is the four-way roman-à-clef imbroglio due to her breakup with the poet Alfred de Musset. It started when he put the whole story in his book *The Confessions of a Child of the Century*. Not to be outdone, Sand in turn published another version of the affair, where he appears as Laurent, in her novel *Elle et Lui*. After this appeared the poet's brother, Paul de Musset, also a novelist, produced another book—an unflattering attack on Sand and her treatment of the poet, which was called *Lui et Elle*. As if there wasn't already enough literature on the affair, still another book, a fourth novel, was produced on the subject. This was written by Louise Colet, a poetess in her own right who had once been the mistress of Musset. She titled her book with considerable ingenuity and simplicity: *Lui*. The pictures in these four books provide an extensive gallery of portraits . . . of the writers by themselves as well as of the characters in the books. The four authors embroiled in this farrago—Alfred de Musset, his brother Paul de Musset, Sand, and Louise Colet—have given the world one of the most extensive and conclusive view of writers writing about writers in the history of literature.

Yet other French writers continued the exposés. When Marie Colombier, in her book *Sarah Barnum,* lampooned the famous Sarah Bernhardt, the actress in revenge not only actually horsewhipped the writer but also engaged her current lover, Jean Richepin, to produce in turn a novel in reprisal. This he did, and the work *Marie Pigeonnier* was an uninhibited attack on the woman writer that contained all the horrid things the actress wanted to say about the authoress. It was during this period that Villiers de L'Isle Adam once instituted a ridiculous lawsuit against a dramatist because he thought a play had vilified a remote ancestor, but he was non-suited. Again, Anatole France admitted that he portrayed the poet Verlaine in the character of Choulette in his work *The Red Lily*. In his work *Penguin Island* he not only made his penguins talk like people but he made them recognizable as his friends, acquaintances, and of course, his enemies. France (whose real name was Jacques Anatole Thibault) included many people in his books, then was himself pen-pointed in Marcel Proust's monumental work *Remembrance of Things Past,* where he shows up as the character Bergotte, while Jean Cocteau is reportedly the character Octave. In this work Proust was said to have killed many birds with this one stone for it includes "pictures" of Maurice Barrés, Paul Bourget, Alphonse Daudet, Ernest Renan, and even John Ruskin who, it has been said, influenced Proust's writing.

The virus of using real people for characters infected almost all of the French writers of this era, just as it had the English writers. While Proust was limning other writers, Joris-Karl Huysmans, in his book *À Rebours,* in turn pictured Proust. Also, Edmond Rostand, in *Chantecler,* drew the character of his poet after Robert de Montesquieu who was known, in real life, as "The Peacock," while Henri Lavedan, in *Le Prince d'Aurec,* drew a portrait based on Paul Bourget.

Even the more modern French writers have succumbed to the contagious habit—and have used or been used in the same fashion. When Francis Carcos' book *Les Innocents,* came out in 1916 it became a popular success although it was mainly about low life in Montmarte—and it contained a portrait of Katherine Mansfield and Beatrice Hastings, a leader in the early feminist revolt and the one-time mistress of Amedeo Modigliani. The book shocked the reading public of the times, because the author showed Hastings as a woman who strangled her lover just to find out what it feels like to be a murderer.

One of the most prolific of women story-tellers was the French writer Colette, whose *Gigi* books swept the nation. Since her death some regional historians have traced the character-sources of her books, and Colette, they say, used some two hundred real-life personages, three-fourths of which lived in the same valley in which she grew up. Her biographer states that the tracing was fairly easily done, since the writer used either the real name, or a slightly disguised name, for her characters.

Even modern French literature is filled with examples of this type of realism. Arthur Koestler portrayed André Malraux, as George St. Hilaire, in his book *The Age of Longing,* and in her book *The Mandarins,* Simone de Beauvoir included portraits of Koestler as well as her life-time lover Jean-Paul Sartre and, of course, Albert Camus. For good measure she also pictured her affair with the American writer Nelson Algren, as Lewis Brogan—much to his discomfort, though he also wrote about her.

If any proof were needed to show that other European writers were "seen" in many writers' books it would only be necessary to point to Russia. It is well known now that Fyodor Dostoyevsky, whose rage was said to be cumulative, in his book *The Possessed* drew a cruel caricature of Ivan Turgenev in the character of Karamazov—and then included him in a second book, *The Devils.* Besides using that writer as a model he also put Nikolai Gogol, in the character of Forma Opiskin, in his book *The Village of Stephanchikova,* sometimes known as *The Friend of the Family.*

Some Scandinavian writers "posed" also. It has been reported that the Norwegian Henrik Ibsen expressed surprise that his countryman Bjørnstjerne Bjørnson should feel hurt at the inclusion of himself in the novel *The League of Youth,* and yet he did not eschew the practice but instead included him a second time, in the character of Haakonsson Haakon in his work *The Pretenders.* On the other hand, it is known too that when Ibsen was portrayed in the book *The Paulsen Family* by John Paulsen, the author (evidently a little troubled that he might have gone too far in his likeness) sent a note to Ibsen that he meant no harm—and Ibsen sent back a simple one-word reply: "Scoundrel!"

Yet it was a popular method to gain attention in the literary world—and the technique was widely used. When the Hungarian Ernest Vajda, in his work *The Harem,* made no effort to hide the fact that he wrote a character into his comedy that was a direct "take off" on an older and better-known playwright from his hometown named Ferenc Molnar, it was no surprise to anyone since it was attributable to the "naturalness" of a younger writer trying to "outshine" an older one.

A simple glance at most European literature of this period will show that the practice was widespread. In Germany, the writer Gerhart Hauptmann was portrayed in Thomas Mann's book *The Magic Mountain* in the character of Pieter Peeperkorn. In Denmark, the writer Roma Wilson (the pseudonym of Florence Roma Wilson, or Mrs. Edward J. O'Brien) etched on paper the character of George Brandes, the eminent critic, in her novel *Death of Society*.

In general, parts of Europe in the 'thirties were steeped in a hot boil of deceptive politics, ideological craziness, and reckless—even dangerous—literature. One of these occasions took place when the author Roderick Guttenbrunn, in his novel *Riff Raff*, drew such a merciless satire of the singer Maria Jeritza and her husband that she prosecuted the writer and had him jailed for a month. And when the Dutch historian/biographer Emil Ludwig wrote a book about Richard Wagner (who had been dead for a century), the work stirred up a hornets' nest to such an extent that a lawsuit resulted. One newspaper critic presumed to criticize the work, and the sensitive author, who had called Wagner every vile name in the lexicon, invoked the aid of the law to protect himself. On the international scene, Francis Beeding—a pseudonym for the collaborators John Palmer and Hilary Saunders—in *The Six Proud Walkers* lampooned Benito Mussolini in the portrait of Caffarelli, the Italian premier in the book, and suffered no consequences. But the German writer Lion Feuchtwanger, in his novel *Success*, presented the early life of Adolph Hitler, especially the Munich episodes, and because of the book he was for a time imprisoned in a concentration camp in France when that country fell to the Nazis in 1940.

VI
America's Hey! Days

WITH the many examples from England and the continent to show the way, it is perhaps perfectly natural that American writers not only followed in their predecessors' footsteps but even tried, in the matter of using real people for their books, to outdo them. At any rate, it was something like a chorus of echoes had crossed the Atlantic—and none of them faint or distant because of the travel. Perhaps a more fitting simile would be that seemingly a virus had crossed the water to infect almost the whole body of American writers—as a glance at even the earliest literature will show.

One of the earliest authors to use this method was Nathaniel Hawthorne who put Margaret Fuller, almost bodily, into his work *The Blythedale Romance*. After he had published *Twice Told Tales* he joined Brook Farm, a noted communal literary colony of the day. Although he remained for a year he had little in common with, and little sympathy for, his brother writers who were also there. Just how little, and exactly what, he thought of them (as well as Margaret Fuller) can be seen in his *Blythedale* book, since he used the whole crowd as character-material for his novel. Also, he put some real people in his other works—he told tales in which the Puritans of New England figured prominently. His own wife is said to have frequently denied that she was

"Hilda" in her husband's work *The Marble Faun,* but it has been suggested that the denials were so frequent that there must have been some likeness. . . .

Another writer, Henry James, put both his sister and his cousin, Mary Temple, in his work *The Wings of the Dove,* while it is believed that Elizabeth Peabody, one of Salem's famous Peabody sisters, was used as the model for Miss Birdseye in *The Bostonians.* (The Peabodys, seemingly, were rich ore for authors to mine. Elizabeth's sister, Sophia, was Hawthorne's wife.)

Henry James, like George Bernard Shaw in England, was something of a bridge between the nineteenth and twentieth century and, like Shaw, included many authorial personalities in his work. He portrayed Mrs. Humphrey Ward (as Mrs. Highmore) in his story "The Next Time" (that later appeared in his book *Embarrassments*) that pictured the successful novelist. He did the same thing to his friend Edith Wharton, showing her in the character of Amy Evans in his story "The Velvet Glove" that later appeared in his book *The Finer Grain.* He also included Samuel Taylor Coleridge in a story, "The Coxon Fund," simply because he had read a biography of the other author. And, like others who also used the technique, he came in for some picturing himself. This was in the story "Lady Tal," which later appeared in the book *Vanities* written by Violet Paget under the pseudonym of Vernon Lee. It has been reported that she took this method of getting even with James for his cool reception of a previous work of hers entitled *Miss Brown.*

In 1903 a little-known but vitriolic book, entitled *The Literary Guillotine,* appeared in the United States. The author, presumably an American, did not use a pseudonym, but left the work unsigned—for very obvious reasons. The work was a witty satire on both American and English authors—taking to task such eminents as Bliss Carmen, Marie Corelli, Ella Wheeler Wilcox, Sir Alfred Austin, Hall Caine, Clinton Scollard, Winston Churchill (the American author, not the British Prime

Minister), Booth Takington, Charles Major, Irving Bacheller, Richard Harding Davis, John Kendrick Bangs, James Brander Mathews, Mrs. Humphrey Ward, Edwin Markham, Henry James, and a whole host of others less well known. While cleverly humorous, the book was nevertheless bitingly satirical and almost libelous in its attacks. It purported to be "an authorized report of the proceedings before the literary Emergency Court holden in and for the District of North America"—for which the reporter was left unlisted. The Bench was shown to be occupied by Mark Twain, Oliver Herford, and one "myself," supposedly the author, while the prosecutor was Charles Battell Loomis. Accordingly, the work was supposed to represent the accounts of the "trials" of authors who had been hauled into court on the charge that "there should be an investigation of all writers whom literature would be better off without. . . ." The book contained many opinions that sparked and glowed concerning those burned in its pages. Though amusing now, at the time of its appearance the work was a bold effort, and it can very well be understood why the author chose to remain anonymous, for not only was Richard Harding Davis roughly treated, and Hall Caine tricked, Mrs. Humphrey Ward was so insulted that an international "incident" almost took place.

The work was a fitting introduction to the part that modern American literature was to play on this stage, for it too can be seen to share in the parade of authors who, either in their own work or someone else's, stride up the steps of the guillotine either to be beheaded or to act as the executioner and lash others to the beheading block. Something of this distinction belongs to Amy Lowell. Following in the footsteps of her kinsman James Russell Lowell, who wrote *A Fable for Critics,* Amy also took many sly digs at her contemporaries. In her book, in which she even paraphrased the other's title *(A Critical Fable)*—which was not signed when it first appeared—Amy attempted, in the manner of Dryden, Swift, Pope, and Lowell to throw the literary spies off the track by including an estimate of her own work. The preface, while not as interesting as the main body of the work, nevertheless gives an indication of the type of things she said about her brother poets:

Sixty odd year ago, a volume appeared
Called *A Fable for Critics,* wherein were ensphered
Eighteen authors of merit. The poet who selected them
Dared many sly prods just because he respected them . . .
In the volume before you, you will find twenty-one
Modern poets popped off 'twixt a laugh and a pun . . .

The twenty-one poets, including herself, were Robert Frost, A.E. Robinson, Carl Sandburg, Edgar Lee Masters, Vachel Lindsay, Hilda Doolittle, Conrad Aiken, John Gould Fletcher, Sara Teasdale, Grace and Hilda Conkling, Alfred Kreymborg, Louis and Jean Untermeyer, Ezra Pound, T.S. Eliot, Maxwell Bodenheim, Wallace Stevens, Edna St. Vincent Millay, and William Rose Benét.*

In this company there was an assortment of writers who were well known at the time. Chief among these were Jack London, who pictured George Sterling (as Russ Brissenden) in his book *Martin Eden* (1909), which showed Sterling's admiration for Ambrose Bierce, and also, perhaps, had a drastic effect

---

*Parodies, as we have seen in English literature, have provided many interesting and amusing instances of literary criticism, generally hiding behind broad or exaggerated humor. In American literature it is possible to find a long list of writers using the technique, from Bret Harte mimicking other writers in his *Nonsense Novels* to James Thurber who aped Erskine Caldwell's Jukes families who were caricatures in themselves, along with Hemingway's parody of Sherwood Anderson's *Dark Laughter* in his own *Torrents of Spring.* In addition there would be writers like Norman Mailer, Tennessee Williams, Edward Albee, Saul Bellow, and J.D. Salinger—all of whom used the technique on others or had it used on them.

on Sterling: the book showed Brissenden committing suicide, and so did Sterling—seventeen years later.

But, keeping London company was another contemporary compatriot: Frank Norris, in his work *The Octopus* (1901), included a portrait of Edwin Markham (as Presley). The writer Hamlin Garland was portrayed by novelist Henry Blake Fuller (as Abner Joyce) in the book *Under the Sky Lights* (1901)—which perhaps was natural since both men were active in the beginning Chicago school of regional realism at the turn of the century.

Keeping them company was William Sydney Porter (O. Henry) who once based a character, Hastings Beauchamp Morley in his story "The Assessor of Success," on another author, Wilson Mizner—who in turn had a disagreeable experience with George Bronson Howard when they collaborated on such plays as *Alias Jimmy Valentine, The Deep Purple,* and *The Greyhound*. Howard, who had borrowed the name Bronson from the more famed playwright, was often erratic. When he got into a scrape with the law Mizner produced his bail and—though Howard fled the country—got the case against him dismissed. Upon his return to the United States the willful and wayward Howard immediately wrote a novel, *God's Man,* in which he proceeded to libel the judge before whom he had appeared. He was rash enough to use real names, which he scribbled onto the proofs. As a result of this the publishers were forced to pay $20,000 damage. Mizner's own reward for befriending the author was just as surprising: Howard next wrote a novelette for the old *Smart Set* magazine called *The Parasite*. Copies of the issue in which the work appeared were recalled by the publisher when Mizner complained, and those never recovered are now very rare. The principal character of the work was called Milton Lazard, and the piece, poisonous from beginning to end, contained libel of the worst sort.

There are, however, some occasions when these affairs have had their comic and humorous aspects, as when Winston

Churchill (the American writer) in his book *The Celebrity* made a satirical hit at the personality of Richard Harding Davis, and said in one of his passages, " 'The Celebrity' is still writing books of a high moral tone and irreproachable principle, and his popularity is undiminished." Also on record is the case of an author who had not offended anyone by putting another author in his work—in the matter of impugning anyone, at least—but nevertheless received blame and condemnation for it. This happened to Charles Reade when his book *The Terrible Temptation* was received with virulent denunciation, and even stigmatized as "carrion literature"—but the book's, or the author's, only fault was that no one had been portrayed in it but the writer.

One of the United States' leading literary personalities, Theodore Dreiser, often embarrassed his friends—even the ones he liked and who liked him—by putting very personal things about them in his books. It is well known, of course, that his book *Sister Carrie,* is the life story of his own sister. Even in such a supposedly innocuous book as *A Traveler,* he depicted with blazing frankness the street-walkers and other women he encountered and associated with, including respectable individuals who were not even thinly disguised. When editor Grant Richards read the script he said, "I have discovered that George Moore at his frankest was, compared to Dreiser, the essence of discretion. No confidence was sacred, no actual, or imagined, secret respected." He also said he shuddered as he read the work that limned even the friends in whose home he had been invited and allowed to bring Dreiser as a guest.

Dreiser's most revealing use of real people (besides the well-known lifting of newspaper accounts of the murder he used as the basis of his book *An American Tragedy*) is apparent in his work *A Gallery of Women,* published in 1915, consisting of fifteen stories that epitomized his kiss-and-tell technique wherein he announced his opinions of couples as well as the women he had loved. In fictionized form he made devastating appraisals of many intimate and close friends. In it he presented his evaluations of Edward and Edith Smith, Hutchins Hapgood, Mary Pyne, and Harry Kemp. Surprisingly, considering the tempo of the times and the tendencies of writers to stridently announce in their books the jealousies, hates, loves, and bitterness that existed between many writers and often motivated them to creative energy, Dreiser's book did not incubate any sort of reprisal, or even a reply, in return. In fact, the opposite occurred. One of the stories, "Roma Martha," was Dreiser's answering portrait to one that Arthur Henry had made of him (Dreiser) in his book *Island Cabin* (1904) that showed all of Dreiser's eccentric waspishness. Evidently, rancor as well as remembrance can live for a long time in a writer's mind.

The 1920s and '30s in American literature was a period that perhaps can best be characterized with the one word, "Hey!" Because the period started at a time when it seemed that anything—everything—was possible, that there was no end to the good times enjoyed by all, and that nothing but expansive growth was the lot of the United States in all areas (despite the term "Lost Generation," which turned out to be a term only and not a fact or reality), literature became more and more vibrant, robust, and vital in every sense—to the point of (sometimes) being shocking. In retrospect it now seems only natural that literature should reflect the era, and the writers reflect the times.

Thus it should not be surprising that many writers more and more write their books as if they would not be outdone by their precursors. And, for some who continued the practice of exposure of their literary friends, relatives, or competitors, it often appeared that, in addition to trying to denude their "characters," they also seemed to be trying to outstrip their predecessors. In view of today's stringency in the laws of libel, it is somewhat astonishing to note how many well-known authors have docilely submitted to the practice and/or used almost direct portraiture in return. Though a risky business, many authors have put caricature in print, and almost as many have made no protest, or did no more than to reply in like manner against their "exposers."

While some books of fiction containing portraiture were not written for the purpose of maligning or ridicule, more often than not many such books were of a damaging nature. This was very apparent in such works as Ellen Terry's *Story of My Life*, in which she accused William Black of putting her in his book *Madcap Violet*. Brander Mathews also accused Black of portraying him in the same book, and explained in his own work *These Many Years* that Black, in revenge for a fancied slight, had pictured him in the novel as "Professor Maunder Bathos." But there is also another side to this story of people in books. Albert Bigelow Paine, in *The Bread Line,* pictured himself and Irving Bacheller, and there were no reverberations. Also, Rose Wilder Lane, in *He Was a Man* (1925), portrayed in a mixture of biography and fiction the life of Jack London, while Samuel Hopkins Adams wrote a satirical dénouement, in *Success,* of a well-known newspaper publisher and his chief editorial writer that can be recognized as William Randolph Hearst and Arthur Brisbane—and again there was no echo of discord.

The listing of such instances could be almost interminable. Harry Kemp, in his book *Love Among the Cape-Enders,* characterized Eugene O'Neill and George Cram Cook, as well as the whole assembly of geniuses that made up the Provincetown Players group. Edna Ferber, in *They Brought Their Women,* wrote of Manhattan during the dizzy 'twenties and certain people to such an extent that it elicited from author Nunnally Johnson the scathing remark that "this authoress has used almost everybody for fictional purposes except Senator Smoot." Isabel Paterson portrayed Will Cuppy in her work *The Golden Vanity,* while Margery Latimer, in *We Are Incredible,* used Zona Gale as the model for a character. Susan Glaspell's play *Alison's House* is based on the life and character of Emily Dickinson, while Helen Hunt Jackson's book *Mercy Philbrick's Choice* was a fictional biography of the same poetess. At this time, also, Anita Loos' work *But Gentlemen Marry Brunettes* showed Franklin Pierce Adams (the noted columnist FPA) in the portrait of him as Joel Crabtree. As though not to be outdone, and keeping the women company in this respect, was Conrad Aiken, who included a picture of Malcolm Lowry in his book *A Heart For the Gods of Mexico,* and William Faulkner, who put his friend Sherwood Anderson in his work *Mosquitoes.* No bad feelings or recriminations of any sort evolved from the portraiture in these books.

The other side of the picture, however, gives a different view. While author Edmund Wilson utilized people wholesale, so to speak, he did not aim to hurt anyone—especially in his work *I Thought of Daisy,* where the character Rita Cavanagh is seen as Edna St. Vincent Millay, and the character Hugh Bamman is John Dos Passos. But Wilson could be damning—and was so in the characterization of a young novelist in his play *The Crime in the Whistler's Room,* in which he achieved revenge on F. Scott Fitzgerald for what he believed to be a characterization of himself in that novelist's book *The Beautiful and Damned.* It was Wilson who startled the New York literary world with his book *Memoirs of Hecate County,* in which he poked vicious satire at some of the so-called guiding lights of the publishing world. Though somewhat camouflouged, many characters in the book could be identified. The work was haled into court, and it was banned—but on the grounds of its lewdness rather than any revelations about people.

To show that Edmund Wilson was not the only writer of this time to point a satirical finger and show up the foibles of the illustrious literary stars, it is only necessary to mention that he was accompanied in this by Max Ewing who, in *Going Somewhere,* made especial capital of Carl Van Vechten and his circle of friends and admirers. At the same time, of course, Van Vechten caricatured not only Fitzgerald but H.L. Mencken in his work *Nigger Heaven,* while in *Peter Whiffle* the character of Edith Dale was copied from Mabel Dodge—who was also a character in George O'Niel's work *American Dream*. All of these occasions had the effect of making American literature something like a roundelay, or round robin—of friends using friends using friends.

In this instance, and because he was one of this country's most talked-about authors, can be placed Alexander Woollcott, who was called "the man who made a reputation from talking about other people."

Long before Moss Hart and George Kaufman lampooned him in the obnoxious house-guest Sheridan Whiteside in their play *The Man Who Came to Dinner* (1939)—reputedly based on Moss Hart's real experience with Woollcott—he had already been pictured, *in toto*, by Charles Brackett in his book *American Colony*. About this, the man who talked about others was forced to say about himself:

"I can scarcely avoid acknowledging as a portrait the somewhat noxious behemoth who passes through that extraordinary novel from pages 169 to 172. This is a tremendous man with tiny extremities and gold-rimmed glasses who used to be a drama critic. He is further described as a competent old bore with a style that is either clear treacle or pure black bile. A sample of that style is then given which, if it is not a forgery, is a damned clever original."

In another book, *Entirely Surrounded,* Brackett continued the portraiture of Woollcott, and this time he generously included his circle of friends, chief among them Noel Coward, who can be seen in the character of Nigel Faraday. Not to be outdone, Daniel McCloud, in his novel *Dance Out the Answer,* lampooned both Woollcott and Carl Sandburg as characters in his book. Even in the field of drama, Woollcott was parodied by his author friends. Samuel N. Behrman's *Brief Moment* included a character that is unmistakably Woollcott, while George S. Kaufman and Moss Hart as collaborators lampooned him in *The Man Who Came to Dinner*—basing the whole drama on a character modeled after Woollcott. To top the masquerade, Woollcott took the part of himself on the stage, as he had earlier in Behrman's play, where he was depicted as a lounging diletante. (Little known by the world at large, however, is that Kaufman and Woollcott were collaborators on the novel *Dark Tower*.) Kaufman and Moss Hart, however, were writers well known for using real people as characters in their work. Along with Woollcott they used Gertrude Lawrence, and in their play *Merrily We Roll Along* they used Dorothy Parker as the model for the character Julia Glenn. She, like Woollcott, also literally took the part of herself on the stage.

At the time of its appearance, the play *Light Up the Sky* was reported as an exposé of the life of Billy and Eleanor Rose, as well as sundry other literary lights including, of course, the author Moss Hart. While the reports and rumors were categorically denied, there were many reasons why they should have been given more than ordinary credence. When it was first hinted that Hart was writing his play about the Roses, and that it would portray them, Walter Winchell said that the playwright's attorney had been warned to caution the author about "toning it down." After the Roses had seen it, Billy wrote in one of his columns all the reasons why he thought the main character could not be him at all, but on the other hand must be several projections of the author himself. That there must have been some truth to the reports that the Roses were limned was psychologically verified by Billy Rose's reaction. His criticism of the play (which he called "Louse Up the Sky") was that it was "a cartoon etched in acid," "a labor of libel," and he referred to its author as having "kinks that irked his id." In other words, Billy Rose reacted to Hart's play as other people have reacted when portrayed in literary works. He was damned annoyed.

Highlighting one Broadway season, authors Samuel and Delia Spewack, in their play *Clear All Wires* lampooned the famous war correspondent Floyd Gibbons, and Edna Ferber and George Kaufman, in their play *The Royal Family,* drew upon the characters of the Barrymore family for their inspiration. In another venture, *Dinner at Eight,* they again lampooned several theatrical bigwigs. Also represented on the stage with literary allusions was Dorothy Parker, appearing in such plays as Philip Barry's *Hotel Universe,* Ruth Gordon's *Over Twenty-One,* John Van Druten's *The Voice of the Turtle,* as well as the work by George Oppenheimer *Here Today.* (Once, when she was asked when she was going to write her autobiography, Parker replied characteristically that she was afraid to because Gordon and Oppenheimer might sue her for plagiarism.)

The writer who shares with Alexander Woollcott the distinction of being the most-written-about or represented person in fiction in American writing is Elinor Wylie. William Rose Benét (her husband), in his work *First Person Singular,* portrayed her and himself and included Sinclair Lewis for good measure. Nancy Hoyt (Elinor Wylie's sister) based a character upon the poetess in her work *Bright Interval,* while Anne Parrish, in *All Kneeling,* drew in the character of Christabel Caine a recognizable portrait—as did Isa Glenn in *East Side of Eden,* which included, besides Wylie, such literary lights as Ford Madox Ford, the authoress herself, and (again) Dorothy Parker—the only female writer who shared with Wylie the spotlight of literary representation. In turn Elinor Wylie was not averse to using recognizable people in her works. In her book *Mr. Hodge and Mr. Hazard* she depicted Lord Byron, Leigh Hunt, and Thomas Babington Macaulay. In her book *The Orphan Angel* she portrayed Shelley, whom she showed as not dying in a shipwreck but crossing the Atlantic and becoming an apparition of liberty in the United States. Other poets, like Wylie, were also not averse to using their friends or acquaintances. Witter Bynner's work *Pins for Wings* skewered many of his contemporaries in two lines apiece, while John Gould Fletcher, in his book *The Black Rock* used Thomas Hardy for a model.

Continuing the tradition as set by earlier novelists, Stephen

Vincent Benét, in *Young People's Pride,* utilized John Chipman Farrar, the former editor of *The American Bookman,* as a model, while in *The Wife of the Centaur,* Cyril Hume used Stephen Benét as the model for Ben Vincent, and used Farrar again, this time as the character of Johnny Chapman. The list of "used" people continued. Katherine Brush fashioned the hero of her novel *Young Man of Manhattan* after the youthful Westbrook Pegler—picturing him in an innocuous portrait as a happy-go-lucky newspaper reporter. Laurence Saunders, in *The Columnist Murder,* depicted a "Tommy Twitchell" whose mellifluous name is not only a derivation of Walter Winchell but makes one suspect that he used the real columnist for a model.

During this period, too, some well-known modern books were produced as outgrowths of dislike, or feuds, between certain authors, and, of course, were written expressly to denigrate or flay the despised opponent. In this manner Maxwell Bodenheim and Ben Hecht, who had collaborated on the play *The Master Poisoner* attempted to poison the public about each other in their literary works. Both men were particularly virulent in their disagreements and about each other, and did not hesitate to indulge their "poisonalities." Bodenheim attacked Hecht first in his book *Ninth Avenue* (1926), in which Hecht appears as Ben Helgrin. Hecht retaliated with his book *Count Bruga* (1926). To this, Bodenheim countered with *Duke Herring* (1931), to which Hecht replied with *A Jew In Love* that lambasted Bodenheim. Some thought the "feud" was staged.

Ben Hecht's wife was also a writer whose work the critics generally did not approve, and showed it in a round-about way; It has been said that Ben Hecht's books were imitations of other writers' tales and styles, and that the style of Rose Hecht (Ben's wife) was an imitation of Ben's imitations. Her work *Women on the Balcony* told her story of meeting with Hecht, their affair, the break-up of his first marriage, and all the same material Hecht had used in two novels and a play.

In the early 1920s the best-known novelist in America was probably F. Scott Fitzgerald, who in the first two years of the decade produced two best-selling books. Fitzgerald, of course, used other writers as models in his work. In one of his best known books, *The Great Gatsby* (1926), he used Ring Lardner (as Owl Eyes)—and did it again (but as Abe North) in his book *Tender Is the Night* (1934). The earliest use of roman à clef by Fitzgerald was in his early book *The Beautiful and the Damned* (1922), wherein he portrayed George Jean Nathan (as Maury Noble) when he was the drama editor for the *American Mercury* magazine. Even earlier than this—which shows that Fitzgerald was not only familiar with but used the technique of roman à clef much more extensively than is generally known—he portrayed the poet John Peale Bishop (as Thomas Parke D'Invilliers) in his book *This Side of Paradise* (1920). And what is not generally known is that Fitzgerald also used Ernest Hemingway (as the model for Philippe) in his *Count of Darkness* stories.

From what can be seen from what has gone before, it was only natural that Fitzgerald should appear in a book also. The first was in Carl Van Vechten's book *Parties* (1930), which presents a picture of him and Zelda (as David and Rilda Westlake). Following him Thomas Wolfe portrayed Scott (as Hunt Conroy) in his work *You Can't Go Home Again* (1940). And following him was Budd Schulberg who, in his book *The Disenchanted* (1950), portrayed Fitzgerald (as Manley Holliday) in the most detailed picture of all.

One of the leading American novelists who used real people for his characters, though little realized by the general public, was Ernest Hemingway. During his early writing career he several times used this method with his acquaintances as models. Hemingway's latest biographer, James Mellows, in his 1992 book,* states near the start of his work (page 22) that early in his

---

*Hemingway, *An Inconsequential Life*—Houghton-Mifflin.

career E.H. was not averse to using real people, and he cites how Marceline Hemingway (E.H.'s sister), to whom he had sent a copy of *Three Stories and Ten Poems,* was shocked that E.H. had used the first names of people they knew in a sordid and vulgar story. His earliest sustained use of the technique was in his book *In Our Time* (1924) wherein he attempted a parody of T.S. Eliot, showing him as a bad poet and his wife resorting to the sexual comforts of a girl-friend. While it was almost broad farce it showed the writer, if no one else, that he had a "gift" for this sort of writing. That he actually had a penchant for it was shown in some of his other early works, notably that which appeared in a German periodical where he took spiteful digs at Ezra Pound and Gertrude Stein—both of whom thought he was a friend. Another example of this "penchant" for using people is shown in his story "Mr. and Mrs. Elliott" (1925), based on the American novelist Chad Powell Smith, another ex-patriot also living in Paris. The picture that Hemingway drew was so vile and reprehensible that Smith, in turn, called Hemingway "a contemptible worm." This so aroused Hemingway that he responded in his usual macho bravado manner (that he was cultivating at the time), offering to knock down Smith a number of times.

In his work *Torrents of Spring* (1926), Hemingway took savage swipes at his friend and mentor Sherwood Anderson by parodying the latter's work *Dark Laughter* with satire and scorn. Anderson did not reply to this, but never talked with or associated with Hemingway afterward.

As well known as these cases were, it was not until E.H. wrote *The Sun Also Rises* (1926) that he made full use of this "gift" on all his acquaintances, and this is the novel of roman à clef with which the American public is most familiar. In it he portrayed, and in some instances caricatured, such people as Donald Ogden Steward (as Bill Gordon), Harold Stearns (as Harvey Stone), Lady Duff Twysden (as Brett Ashley), Harold

Loeb (as Robert Cohn), and a host of others including Robert McAlmon (who had published E.H.'s first book), and Ford Madox Ford and his mistress Stella Bowen (as Mr. and Mrs. Braddocks) who might have been accorded more gentle treatment from the hands of one whom Ford had assisted—making him an assistant editor of *Transition*—when E.H. was on his uppers in Paris.

Regardless of his cavalier treatment of his friends, the book was a best-seller and was the making of E.H.'s reputation as a writer. It did not, however, cure him of the habit of writing disparagingly about the people he knew. In his book *To Have and Have Not* (1937), Hemingway again included a bitter portrait of another writer, this time John Dos Passos (as Richard Gordon). The portrait was so vicious that Arnold Gingrich, editor of *Esquire* magazine, asked Hemingway to delete or "tone down" some passages. This Hemingway refused to do, and the portrait remains one of the most vicious and damaging ever printed.

Of course, Hemingway was used in turn, and appeared in many books, not always favorably. Surprisingly, the first was Jean Rhys, which work *Postures* (1928), used E.H. and showed him (as Cairn) in a romantic light. It was withal a faint portrait because Rhys did not know Hemingway and indeed had not even met him. As might be expected, of course, and offsetting the previous picture, was Harold Stearns*—who had been pil-

---

*Practically the only sympathetic appraisal or picture of Harold Stearns occurred in Kay Boyle's novel *Monday Night* (1938) that depicts him as he was in their Paris days of the 'twenties. Her portrait is completely different from the one that Ernest Hemingway drew of him (as Harvey Stone) in *The Sun Also Rises*. Earlier, Boyle drew a picture of Ernest Walsh (as Martin Sheehan) in her book *Year Before Last* (1932) that was a tender, sympathetic revelation of the consumptive poet/editor for whom she had run away from her marriage to live with. Later, Boyle again used some living characters to people her book *My Next Bride* (1934) that depicted Harry and Caresse Crosby (as Anthony and Romaine Lister) that showed them almost as a second Scott-and-Zelda Fitzgerald couple in their pursuit of nothing but pleasure.

loried by E.H. In his book *The Street I Know* (1935) Stearns merely let Hemingway know that his barbs had gone home.

Another woman who put E.H. in her books was Dawn Powell, with whom Hemingway had a long friendship—probably because they did not see each other very often. Powell used E.H. (as the character Andy Callingham) in several novels, picturing him as an internationally known publicity hunter, and a self-satisfied and self-motivated novelist. Hemingway either missed her subtle gibes or felt they weren't worth getting excited about, with the result that the occasional exposures by her pen had no effect on him, and no harsh words were voiced.

Other writers were not so gentle. And where E.H. had used scorn and satire, gibes and devastating criticism on others, he was to suffer some of the savage swipes he had dished out. One of these dénouements was as devastating to him as had, up to then, ever appeared in print. This occurred with the ridicule that "exposed" him as he had exposed others. It came in the form of the book by Albert Halper, *Farewell To the Rising Sun* (1931), which burlesqued not only E.H. himself but all his writings. Of this burlesque it was said, Halper "did a better job on Hemingway than E.H. had done on Anderson (whose *Dark Laughter* had received Hemingway's most vicious ridicule). Besides doing a "job" on E.H. the book thoroughly debunked the "hard-boiled" attitude that Hemingway affected, showing it to be nothing but a pose.

But it was not the end of the Hemingway circus. In 1933 Ford Madox Ford—whom E.H. treated most badly in spite of favors provided him—replied with a portrait of Hemingway in turn. In his book *The Rash Act* (1933), Ford showed the Hemingways (as Mr. and Mrs. Jack Percival) in the early days of his writing life (and included a glimpse of Gertrude Stein, who had claimed she taught E.H. how to write).

When Irwin Shaw's book *The Young Lions* (1948) unfavorably showed an aging war-correspondent with a likeness resembling

Ernest Hemingway, E.H. became indignant, but did nothing about it. Shaw never admitted the portrait—or denied it.

It was not until 1951—fourteen years after being attacked by E.H.—that John Dos Passos answered Hemingway's picture of him in *To Have and Have Not* with his own book *Chosen Country* (1951). In this work Dos Passos drew a portrait of Hemingway (as George Elbert Warner). While it was not too damaging or detrimental of E.H., he nevertheless did it again in a second book, *Century's End* (1975). Perhaps he repeated the picture so that no one would ever forget what Ernest Hemingway was like.

The last novel in which Hemingway appeared as a character was in Maia Rodman's book *The People in His Life* (1980). This showed Hemingway in the agonizing period of his hospital days leading to his suicide. It also exposed his use of women in his life to achieve what he wanted.

All but the last two books were published during Hemingway's life, and strange as it may seem in light of Hemingway's belligerent and hard-boiled attitudes, none of them—except Dos Passos' picture—affected E.H., but slid off his shoulders without so much as a verbal shrug.

A strange coincidence exists between the first and last novels that contain portraits of Ernest Hemingway as a character in a book. The first was written by a writer who did not know him, and so was the last.

Past the 'thirties the storm continued—but now with diminishing loudness and less drenching rain. While the crescendo was over and the actual deluge reduced, the previous flooding slowly seeped away, and only a few isolated occasions reminded of the once prevalent art-form of putting living writers in books as characters. One of the later users was Thomas Wolfe who, in his first book, *Look Homeward Angel* (1929), included a picture of Sinclair Lewis (as Lloyd McHarg). Because it was a favorable one, Lewis championed the book and started Wolfe on his literary career. Because the method seemed so successful to the new author, he used it again in his second novel, the 1940 *You Can't Go Home Again,* and included the same character, with the same name as before.

In 1949 Mary McCarthy, in her book *Oasis,* pictured Dwight McDonald (as the character Macdougal Macdermott), who was the editor of *Partisan* magazine when she was its drama critic.

In 1961, John Cheevers' book *Miscellany of Characters* showed John O'Hara in the character of Hoyden Blake, and in 1962 Herman Wouk, in his book *Youngblood Hawks,* is said to have portrayed Thomas Wolfe as its main character, although he claimed it was Honoré de Balzac he was portraying. The writer Peter DeVries, in his book *Reuben! Reuben!* (1964), pictured the Welsh poet Dylan Thomas (as Gowan McGlade), and Margaret Drabble, in her book *The Waterfall* (1969), depicted the controversial poetess Sylvia Plath. While this work was not a roman à clef *per se,* there were so many occurrences happening both to the model and the character that it is easy to identify the personage by the likenesses.

Many novelists have "exploded" onto the world's scene with a first novel, only to sink back into insignificant work, or no work at all. This happened to John Updike's character Henry Bech in the book *Bech, A Book* (1970). Some in the literary world thought it a picture of many different American novelists, including Capote, Bellows, Malamud, and even Updike himself—who "believed" his character was a Norman Mailer "lookalike." Mailer eventually did actually "appear" (as Jock Hecht) in Roger Simon's work *Wild Turkey* (1975), while Harold Robbins drew a picture of Jacqueline Susann (as Jeri-Lee Randall) in his book *The Lonely Lady* (1976). It appeared two years after Susann's death, and was a flattering memorial to a once-vivacious writer.

Included in the list of later work must be Saul Bellow's book *Humboldt's Gift* (1975) that used the writer Delmore Schwartz as a model. Following him was Louis Auchincloss who, in his book

The House of the Prophet (1980), included a portrait of the famous political columnist Walter Lippmann (as Felix Leitner).

Only a remnant of the flood remained with the publication of Philip Roth's book *The Anatomy Lesson* (1984) that presented a character (Milton Appel) believed to be Irving Howe, the critic who had once derided Roth's work in print. All that Roth would explain, when his book came out, was that he was furious when he wrote the book; furious about being "misunderstood."

While maybe not significant in itself (perhaps it is safe to say that almost all writers—at one time or another—believe or feel that they are "misunderstood"), it also signified the close of an epoch that perhaps will never again be rivaled—or even exist.

VII
The King of the Beats

THE Beat Generation of writers that seemed to have sway over a part of literature during the 'fifties and 'sixties actually was just another incident in the history of literature—and protest. This time, however, it was an explosion of protest that took the form of drug-addiction and alcoholism as a way of life against the status quo, against the "establishment," against all the values of life in the United States. In relying on the use of alcohol and drugs to the point of extinction, the movement turned out to be a total bust, with the possible exception of Kerouac himself whose work remains as an interesting souvenir of an age. It was not the first—nor is it likely to be the last—of such protest movements among writers or literature.

In the 'fifties and 'sixties, the Beat Generation that sprang up did so at first like all outbursts, or protest, with promises of arcana if more of the populace followed or allowed the militant leftists the whole battleground. From all viewpoints, however, it was a strange movement. The irony infesting the "Beats" rested in the condition that infected all of the members—not just casual but excessive alcoholism and drug usage, and the insistence that the salvage of the world depended on such excess. Thus, the activists were their own worst enemy.

Kerouac's position in the movement is rife with strangeness.

He named the movement the Beat Generation, and claimed that the name referred to the "Beatific" generation—but the public immediately grasped the fact that the group he was talking about was, in fact, a "beat" generation all right, since all the characters in the movement (and his books) were a "lost" as well as a "beaten" bunch of misfits who based their existence—and work—in a mission of alcoholism and drug-addiction, while fantasizing with visions of . . . nothingness.

Kerouac was not an organized writer. His sentence structure would range from a gallop in ideas to a canter in ideologies, and then to a trot on stray ideas or a sedate walk on various musings—all interspersed with dashes as the paces changed or veered course. His prose reflected the tenacity of a man with a message, and whose soul struggles to get that message out any way possible. He was not a stylist in any sense of the word, or even an organizer of his words in the sense of that word.

Kerouac's fate as a writer is that he ended up only as an historian of his era, with his strong suit being the glimpses and parades of his followers (his "clan"), with whom he was so enthralled that he tried to put all of them in every book he wrote. Although he ended as a bitter, sour man (he was heard by all but did not affect the pubic he sought to influence or change), he nevertheless became (and remains) the King of the Beats. Today his almost solitary claim to fame rests not on the fact that he was the spokesman and historian of the movement, but on the fact that he also was the biographer of the vocal (literary) members of the movement. The amount of space here devoted to him is not because he was a symbol of the Beat movement, or its most prolific spokesman and historian, but because he was a greater user of roman à clef than any other writer in history.

He did this by putting all his friends, companions, and followers in his books. If any one author can be said to have staked his career on the reproduction in words of all his acquaintances, the accolade must be awarded to Kerouac if only for the sheer numbers alone. More than any other writer in the world's literary history, he peopled his work with characterizations of the real people he knew instead of creating "characters" from his imagination.

The list of people that Kerouac used for his books is a very long one, consisting of forty-two people (or forty-two times he used people, often more than once) who were deliberately manipulated as "copy" for an exercise in "literature." Taken as a whole, it seems that of all the roman à clef writers the world has known (or seen), Kerouac more than any one distorted Bernard Shaw's dictum ("write about what you know") into "write about whom you know." Not surprisingly, this excess has something about it that is a little "off"—as though the author was caught flatfooted at keyhole spying or window-peeping.

In this listing of Kerouac's use of a horde of living writers in his books, it might also be said of him, as was said about Aldous Huxley: either he was so besotted by the people he knew that he had to use them as characters in his books (over and over again), or else he was unable, strictly on his own, to create any characters that could enrich or enliven his books.

In his first book, *The Town and the City*, Kerouac portrayed William Burroughs and his wife Joan (as Will and Mary Dennison), and in this work he also included a picture of Allen Ginsberg (as Leroy Levinsky.)*

Kerouac's second book, *On the Road* (1957), included another portrait of Burroughs (as old Bull Lee) and his wife Joan (as Jane) while the writer Carolyn Robinson was also pictured (as Camille). Besides these, Kerouac used John Clellon Holmes for the model of Tom Saybrook, along with another picture of

---

*Also in this book is a minor character for which, it has been claimed, Ginsberg provided a partial model. When Kerouac was asked why it was such a small part, he said, "Because he's not an interesting character to me. He doesn't do anything but talk."

Ginsberg (as Carlo Marx.) Keeping them company was a portrait of Luanne Henderson (as Marylou) and, for the very first time, Neal Cassady (as Dean Moriarty).

In 1958 Kerouac wrote two books, *The Dharma Bums* and *The Subterraneans*. In the latter he included another picture of William Burroughs (as Jack Carmody) and along with him a portrait of Whit Burnett, the editor of *Story* magazine (as Walt Fitzpatrick). In this work Kerouac, for the second time, used Neal Cassady (as Leroy) and gave us another picture of John Clellon Holmes (as Balliol Mac-Jones). Once more, he pictured Luanne Henderson (as Annie) while of course there was the perennial Ginsberg (as Adam Moorad)—even though he'd said Ginsberg was a wind-bag. Parading through this book are vignettes of Lawrence Ferlinghetti (as Leroy O'Hara) and the novelist William Gaddis (as Harold Sand).

The other 1958 book, *The Dharma Bums,* contains all the now-familiar faces we have met before: here are William Burroughs and his wife Joan (again as Will and Mary Dennison), along with Allen Ginsberg (as Alvah Goldbrook). Not content with this, Kerouac introduces us to some newcomers: Philip Lamantia (as Francis de Pavia), Kenneth Rexroth (as Reinhold Cocoethes), Gregory Corso (as Yuri Gligoric), Michael McClure (as Ike O'Shay), Gary Snyder (as Japhy Ryder), and Neal Cassady (as Cody Pomeroy).

In his book *Visions of Cody* (1960), Kerouac used his old friend Allen Ginsberg once again (now as Irwin Garden,) and we make the reacquaintance of Carolyn Robinson—now Carolyn Cassady—(as Evelyn). Still more oldtimers reappear: John Clellon Holmes (as Tom Wilson), Lawrence Ferlinghetti (as Danny Richman), and of course his major character Neal Cassady (as Cody Pomeroy).

In his 1961 work *The Book of Dreams,* we again meet John Clellon Holmes (as James Watson) and Gregory Corso (as Raphael Urso), along with—of course—Neal Cassady (again as

Cody Pomeroy) and that unforgettable (to Kerouac) oldtimer—Allen Ginsberg (as Irwin Garden again).

In *Big Sur* (1962), Kerouac reacquaints us with some people we thought we already knew: Lawrence Ferlinghetti (as Lorenzo Monsato), Neal Cassady (as Cody Pomeroy), Michael McClure (as Patrick McLear), and—who else?—Allen Ginsberg (in the third version of Irwin Garden).

In *Desolation Angels* (1965), the author shows us his preoccupation with, and the preeminent attention paid to, of all his characters in all his books, Neal Cassady, and his more-or-less automatic reappearance (again as Cody Pomeroy). Here it seems the author is trying to include in his work all his acquaintances, for again we meet Gregory Corso (again as Raphael Urso), Philip Lamantia (as David D'Angeli), Michael McClure (again as Patrick McLear), Robert Duncan (as Geoffrey Donald), Randall Jarrall (as Random Varnum), James Merrill (as Merrill Randall), and Gary Snyder (as Jerry Wagner). Not surprisingly his old friend William Burroughs appears—without his wife—as Bull Hubbard. Surprisingly though, he included a newcomer to his gallery of portraits: Norman Mailer (as Harvey Marker).

Kerouac's last book, *Vanity of Duluoz* (1968), provides the author's faithful readers with the impression that he has been reading the same book over and over—especially since, in this work, Kerouac attempted to consolidate or coalesce all his views, all his opinions, in one volume, and in doing so, of course, reemploy the same people we have seen in his other books. Not only is William Burroughs present (this time as Wilson Holmes), and the indispensable figure of Allen Ginsburg (still as Irwin Garden), but all the others too. In short, one can only come to the conclusion that much of Kerouac's "fiction" is not really fiction at all. In the strictest sense it may be said that much of Kerouac's work suffers from "echolalia"—that same disease that made Gertrude Stein repeat the same words over and over. In his use of the same characters time after time, reading

Kerouac is like hearing one echo after an echo after an echo—*ad infinitum*.

An outstanding fact about the Beat movement is that Kerouac, in delineating the long line of writers in the movement, earned for himself the title of "The King of the Beats,"—and in using them as characters in his books, he became their historian.

A remarkable fact is that of all the writers Kerouac used in his books, not one, not once, complained, replied, or even mentioned his inordinate use of them.

The most astonishing fact of all is that, of the long list of writers that Kerouac used, not one, not once, wrote anything about Kerouac.

VIII
No Private Lives

WHILE it may not seem unusual to see friends and acquaintances at loggerheads, or relatives display the family linen in print, what is astonishing is that even husbands and wives have frequently been accused of picturing and/or ridiculing each other in books.

That husband and wife writers have not confined their differences to the home, the courts, or the judge's chambers is apparent in many books . . . even books that are so-called works of fiction, novels, and short stories. Though passing as "fiction," many of the works of this type that a surprising number of writers have turned out are in reality more than that—they are out-and-out true stories.

One of the first American writers to depict a wife as a character in a book was Henry Brooks Adams—scion of the famous Adams family of Boston, whose literary accomplishments started when John Adams had a lengthy correspondence with his wife Abigail. Henry Brooks Adams, in his work *Esther* (1884), portrayed his wife Marian (as Esther Dudley). It was among the first—if not *the* first—book in this country that was a complete picture of a wife by a writer. Although entirely favorable in tone, assessment, and consideration about the subject, it did not augur or even set a precedent for writing favorably about a wife.

For in the work of writers of both sexes we can see, in holding their "day in court" in print between covers—with the world to act as their judge and jury, and each writer performing as his own attorney—why many have been frequently accused of deliberately ridiculing their spouses in their work.

This was true of novelist Arthur Stringer, whose wife divorced him on those grounds; and it was true of Edgar Lee Masters, the Kansas poet and author of *Spoon River Anthology,* who was accused of the same thing.

To note that wives have done the same to husbands, it is only necessary to point to Natalie Sedgwick Colby, a novelist also, who calumniated her husband in a book—even though he was an ex-Secretary of State. Again, we can see Edith Wharton put her faithless, philandering husband in her novel *The Age of Innocence,* where she depicted him in the character of Bron Olenski. And—even for the opposite reasons—wives have been displayed just as blatantly but in a different light, as when William Rose Benét portrayed his wife, Elinor Wylie, in his novel *First Person Singular,* a work wholly flattering so that, of course, the writer-wife could not take exception to it.

Sinclair Lewis had more than most writing man's trouble with a writing wife, although he should have known what he was letting himself in for when he married another writer. When his first marriage to Grace Hegger Lewis broke up, she published a novel, *Half a Loaf,* which was described by one reviewer as "splitting the hair between fiction and fact almost to the vanishing point." Already separated when the work appeared, there were no further or outward repercussions over the work, but when Lewis married Dorothy Thompson, the world-renowned foreign correspondent, it is possible to find that it is Sinclair Lewis who is doing all the writing about the marriage. In his book *Dodsworth* (1929) he included Dorothy (as Edith Cortland) and also provided the world with another view of his first wife (as Fran Voelker). Seemingly not content with this, he did it all a second time in his book *Gideon Plannish* (1943), where he pictured Dorothy (as Winifred Homeward) in a portrait that was not a gentle one but contained so many satirical jabs at his ex-mate that it was mostly caricature.

Of all the prominent American authors who used their wife as models for a book character, F. Scott Fitzgerald, in the matter of number of times, ranks with the records of Ernest Hemingway and Sinclair Lewis. Zelda appears in three of his stories, and three of his novels. Her first appearance (as Sally Carol Happers) is in the story "The Ice Palace," later included in his book *Flappers and Philosophers* (1920). He repeated the picturing of her (as Gloria Patch) in his novel *The Beautiful and the Damned* (1922). He did it again in his story "The Sensible Thing," this time as Jonquil Cary, which appeared in his book *All the Sad Young Men* (1926), and of this work Scott explained: "It's about Zelda and me. All true." In another story, "One Trip Abroad," included in his book *Afternoon of an Author* (1930), Zelda appears (as Luella Kelly), and does so yet again (as Nicole Diver) in the novel *Tender Is the Night*—although it is believed by some critics to be only a partial picture. Her last appearance in one of Fitzgerald's books was as Minna Stahr in his book *The Last Tycoon* (1941). It is a record that is almost as long and complete as that of D.H. Lawrence, or Ernest Hemingway, or Sinclair Lewis.

Zelda (of course) in turn wrote about Scott. With her somewhat fey personality and oftentimes lack of any sense of consequence, the only thing that could ever be expected of her was the unexpected. And this she did with her novel *Save Me the Waltz* (1932). Scott was favorably impressed with her accomplishment, but also chagrined at the portraiture of himself. His resentment was based—since the work was largely a disclosure of their relationship as husband and wife—on her critical picture of the main male character that was recognizably patterned on him, and because she had, apparently, deliberately competed with his own style of writing by copying it.

Ernest Hemingway was another writer who put his wives in his books. He did not obviously include his first wife Hadley in any of his works although Scott Fitzgerald says that he did. But starting with his second the situation changes—for in his work *The Green Hills of Africa* he portrayed Pauline Pfeiffer. Later, in his work *The Fifth Column,* he portrayed his third wife, Martha Gellhorn, in the character of Dorothy Bridges, picturing her down to the details and idiosyncrasies, such as her profession (war correspondent), the same kind of looks, educational background, domestic qualities, hygienic habits, and even the eccentricity of always favoring the wearing of a silver-fox cape. It has also been said that she was partly the model for the character of Maria in his book *For Whom the Bell Tolls.* So far as women in his books were concerned, it was Morley Callaghan, in his work *That Summer in Paris,* who said that Scott Fitzgerald had Hemingway pegged right when it came to equating the two—that he had a theory about Hemingway's women and his books. He said, "Ernest needs a woman for each book. There was one for his stories and *The Sun Also Rises.* There's Pauline (Pfeiffer the second wife) and *A Farewell to Arms,* a big book. If there's another I think you will find Ernest has another wife." In substantiation of this "theory" we only have to look at the record: in *The Green Hills of Africa* (1935) he introduced us to Pauline Pfeiffer, his second wife. In *For Whom the Bell Tolls* (1940) we meet Martha Gellhorn (a writer in her own right). In his later books *Across the River* and *Into the Trees* (1950) we meet Mary Welsh, his fourth and last wife. It was she, after Hemingway's death in 1961, who had the courage to bring out his book of memoirs—*A Moveable Feast* (1964)—which gave almost a chapter and verse listing of other women in his life.

Gertrude Stein was somewhat acidulous in her remark equating E.H. and his books. Apropos of his marriages she said: "A man who marries three women from St. Louis evidently didn't learn much." (It is also a statement that very easily can be translated to: "A man who marries three writers evidently didn't learn much.")*

Only one of his wives ever wrote anything about Hemingway. That was Martha Gellhorn who, in her novel *The Stricken Field* (1940), included Hemingway (as John) and herself (as Mary Douglas) as the main characters. It was an innocuous work, dealing with their experiences in the Spanish civil war and not—for once—a descriptive battle between the characters. But after the divorce it was Martha who gave the more succinct and concise summation of E.H.: "Papa Hemingway has no redeeming qualities outside of his writing."

Among the strange examples of this type of character-drawing may be mentioned William Faulkner's use of his wife Estelle (as Cicily) in his first book, *Soldier's Pay*, which portrays her as he saw her before they were married. At the end of his career, Faulkner was pictured in Joan Williams' novel *The Wintering*, which exposed their affair: at age fifty-two, a writer unable to conduct the type of love affair wanted and expected by a thirty-year-old mistress.

Even more strange was Malcolm Lowry's book *Dark Is the Grave Wherein My Friend Is Laid* (1969), in which he depicted (as Primrose Wilderness) his wife Margerie Bonner Lowry—a novelist in her own right—who shared his penurious and nomadic life in the United States, Mexico, Sicily, France, and England.

Perhaps the strangest and certainly the most exotic of all the books written about a wife, however, was John Berryman's *Homage To Mistress Bradshaw*, wherein he so used his wife, the short story writer and novelist Eileen Simpson, that she acknowledged her life was entwined with that of the colonial poetess (1612-72) to such an extent that it was difficult to distinguish between them.

*Pauline Pfeiffer worked for the Paris office of *Vanity Fair;* Martha Gellhorn worked for *Collier's* magazine; Mary Welsh worked for the Paris office of Time-Life, Inc.

The English writers were as addicted to this habit as the American writers. As we have seen earlier, Mary Shelley was among the first, if not the first, to put a spouse in her work. She did this in her first book, *Lodore,* portraying Shelley (as Adrian). She did it again in her second book, *The Last Man* (1826), and for good measure included a picture of Byron along with the picture of her husband.* But, the woman writer who qualifies to wear the crown for most such portrayals was Lady Lytton, the wife of Lord Edward Bulwer-Lytton, the author of *The Last Days of Pompeii.* As a writer this man seemed to have a genius for arousing the antagonism of his fellow authors, and his wife, even after they were divorced, wrote many novels in which she raged against and about him—all designed, of course, to put him in an unfavorable light in the public eye. Among other things, she habitually called him "Sir Liar."

In the listing of books and authors that depict wives and husbands, very often the relationship is apt to be between paramours rather than married people—and is there any reason to believe that such portrayals are not as accurate a drawing "to the life" as one between married enemies?—it should not surprise that the list includes some of the world's best known and/or famous writers. But all of them, while not always exoteric in their relations, have nevertheless used and followed in the footsteps that much earlier had been tracked all over the landscape. As we have seen, George Bernard Shaw appeared in the work of his mistress Florence Farr, who depicted him (as George Travers) and their seven-year affair in her book *The Dancing Faun* (1894). To this Shaw responded by limning her (as Grace Tranfield) in his work *Philanderers* (1898)—and even earlier than that (as Louka) in his work *Arms and the Man* (1894).

*Mary Shelley, by putting him as a character in her book, gave Byron the honor of appearing in one of the world's first (if not *the* first) sci-fi novel. What is not so generally known is that Shelley, himself, in 1818, also penned a portrait of Byron in his book *Julian and Maddolo.*

At about this time George Gissing pictured his wife (as Ada Peachy) in his book *The Year of the Jubilee* (1894), and following him was Violet Hunt (in picturing her mostly-absent husband, the writer Oswald Crawford, as Ralph Assheton) in her book *Sooner or Later* (1904).

Probably among the world's best-known writers who wrote about women was D.H. Lawrence, whose tangled love affairs not only gave him material for his books but provided his partners with material to write about him. In his book *The Trespasser* (1912), he portrayed an early love for Helen Corke, whom he called Helena Verden in his book. It was an unhappy affair for both of them and when it was over she, in her novel *Neutral Ground* (1933), portrayed Lawrence (as Derrick Hamilton).* In his book *The Fight For Barbara,* Lawrence depicted his affair with Frieda Weekley, the wife of Professor Ernest Weekley (pictured as Dr. Frederick Tressider) before she left her husband and ran away with D.H.L. After he married Frieda, Lawrence put her in at least eight of his books, each time with a different name—the best known as Harriet Somers. She was also pictured in the books of five other writers.†

Lawrence seemingly was chronically unable to keep his friends out of his books, especially the women he knew. While he did not have an affair with Katherine Mansfield, he nevertheless used her several times in his work. (As we have seen, he included her in *The Rainbow* and *Women In Love,* as well as some short stories.) He did this all the while he was involved with other women as well.

*She also wrote two books, *Lawrence and the Apocalypse* (1933) and *In Our Infancy* (1975), relating her experiences with Lawrence.

†As Nelly Olover in Gilbert Canaan's *Mendel* (1916), as Mary Rampton in Aldous Huxley's *Point Counterpoint* (1928), as Hildegarde Rayner in Compton Mackenzie's *South Wind of Love* (1942), as Katy Maartens in Huxley's *The Genius and the Goddess* (1955), and as Elizabeth Frederick in Hilda Doolittle's *Bid Me to Love* (1960). She also appeared in Kay Boyle's story "The Rest Cure" that was included in her book *Thirty Stories* (1948).

In fact, Lawrence could be very Puckish in his relations with women, as his associations with Dorothy Brett and Mabel Dodge Luhan show. These two, along with Frieda whom he was constantly portraying in his books, had a definite bearing on his work, and perhaps influenced it more than is generally known or perceived. Each of them wrote books about him, all proclaiming that they were in love with him; and each of the books, wildly proclaiming it were vociferous and jealous declamations of being the most sympathetic to him and his work. Each book, of course, a was denunciation of the rivals. The three books and their authors were: *Not I, But the Wind,* by Frieda Lawrence (D.H.L.'s wife); *Lorenzo in Taos* by Mabel Dodge Luhan, and *Lawrence and Brett,* by Dorothy Brett. The latter, as subsequent dénouement showed, didn't have a chance, and Mabel Luhan's claims were eventually discredited when Frieda, in her work, was able to produce a letter that Lawrence wrote to his mother-in-law in which he told what he really thought of Mabel.

But these "affairs," four-sided as they were, did not leave Lawrence totally unresponsive or aloof. In a series of short stories he portrayed each of them in turn. In his 1925 story "The Last Laugh," he portrayed Dorothy Brett in the character of Miss James. He pictured her again in the story "The Princess" (first published in the same year as the other), in the character of Dollie Urquhart. He did the same thing to Mabel Luhan. In 1925 he portrayed her in his story "The Woman Who Rode Away" and in his 1926 story "The Glad Ghost," which was not so much a portrayal as a caricature.

All of the stories appeared in the 1928 book titled *The Woman Who Rode Away.* Almost cunningly, however, Lawrence included in this collection a story, "Smiles," written in 1926, in which the character Ophelia is another of his portraits of Katherine Mansfield.*

*Katherine Mansfield, in her story "Je ne parle français," which was published in her 1920 book *Bliss,* wrote of her six-day love affair with François Carco (in

In the matter of numbers, however, D.H. Lawrence wrote about his wife more than any other writer, seemingly almost unendingly. Even in his first book, *The Fight For Barbara* (1912), D.H.L. detailed the events that led to her flight from Professor Weekley to join him in a trip abroad. In this work she appears as Barbara Tressider. Always, thereafter, she seems to have asserted an influence, for in his work *The Rainbow* (1915) Lawrence drew pictures of Louie Burrows (as Ursula, his first love) and Katherine Mansfield (as Gudrun Brangwen)—but there are traces of Frieda in the pictures he drew of all three women when he eloped after breaking his engagement to Louie Burrows. Lawrence's biographer, Emile Delavanay, suggested that Lawrence also partially used Frieda for the character of Lydia Lensky. The three women appear again in his book *Women In Love* (1920).

Frieda appears next in his book *Kangaroo* (1923), where she is portrayed as Harriet Somers—the first complete picture of her that he ever drew. It was to be one of his major works, even outclassing the famous *Lady Chatterley's Lover* (1926) about which, he admitted, the main character was "partly" based on Frieda. She appeared once again in his work *The Plumed Serpent* (1926), wherein he shows her as Kate Leslie—along with a sour and somewhat dyspeptic picture of the American writer Witter Bynner (as Owen Rhys).

In Lawrence's story "The Border Case" that appeared in his 1928 book *The Woman Who Rode Away,* he outlined the affair between Frieda and John Middleton Murry. It has been said that Frieda attempted to live her life as her husband preached (free love) but it was not her last, any more than it was the first, of her infidelities. (Or, if we are to believe Mabel Luhan, et al., his either.)

the character of Raoul Duquette), then returned to her husband, Middleton Murry, disillusioned. She of course appeared (as Winnie) in Carco's book *Les Innocents* (1916).

Frieda's last appearance in Lawrence's work is in his story "Mr. Moon" that appeared in the book *A Modern Lover* (1934), in which he pictured both his mother-in-law, Baroness Von Richthoven, and Frieda. It was something of a "family" portrait.

The last word on the woman-troubled Lawrence was given by his one-time mistress, Hilda Doolittle, who used her former lover for the character Achilles in her 1961 book *Helen of Egypt*. Hilda Doolittle seemingly enjoyed putting all her friends (and lovers) in her books, since she did it all the time. She included Ezra Pound (as George Lowndes) in her book *Hermione* (written in 1927 but not published until 1981), which showed that this entanglement for HD was as disappointing as her other affairs with men (including D.H. Lawrence and Richard Aldington). In her book of memoirs, *End to Tomorrow* (1980), she showed that for her Pound would have been as impossible to live with as he was difficult to live without.

A writer who had almost as complex an association with women as Lawrence, but handled the affairs differently, was Richard Aldington. Because of his three marriages (and his feistiness with his literary friends) he was an author who said much—and did much—in the business of using people in his books. Besides being a novelist he was also a critic and a biographer, and he employed all three talents in all of his work. He so employed his talents that it seemed he was constantly putting all his loves (and his hates) in his books; fortunately, not all in one book.

In his work *Death of a Hero* (1929), Aldington not only included Ford Madox Ford but satirized him in the character of Herr Shobbe. (His description of him was as "a plump, talented snob.") In the same book he painted a vitriolic portrait of Hilda Doolittle (in the character of Elizabeth Waterbourne), who had been Ford's mistress before marrying Aldington. His splenetic attack, of course, was due to his blaming her for the break-up of their marriage (Hilda's and Richard's). Although he drew a merciless picture of her in this book, at the same time he credited her with more subtlety and depth than he accorded to any other Aldington heroine.* And, as if showing off his talent as a biographer at the same time as being a muckraker, Aldington included a picture, in the character of Fanny, of Dorothy Yorke, who was to become his second wife. Again, in his book *All Men Are Enemies,* he included his third wife, Brigit Patmore (in the character of Katha)—as she herself admitted in her 1968 memoirs.

Aldington was at his ferocious and vicious best in his *Death of a Hero* (which in reality is saying a great deal because he flayed D.H.L. alive in his work: *D.H. Lawrence: Portrait of a Genius, But* . . .). As with Ford, Aldington made his personal dislikes and thinly disguised characters well known to the world by the simple expedient of presenting his personal descriptions. He described D.H. Lawrence (who was rumored to be the father of Hilda Doolittle's daughter, Perdita) as a "sandy-haired, narrow-chested little man with spiteful blue eyes and a malevolent class-hatred," who "exercised his malevolence with comparative impunity by trading on his working-class origin and his indigestion, of which he had been dying for twenty years." (The "indigestion," of course, was tuberculosis.) It has been reported that this malevolent picture of Lawrence was written by a pen that dripped malevolence. It has also been reported that Lawrence, when shown portions of this book, said to Aldington: "If you publish this you'll lose what reputation you have—you're plainly on the road to an insane asylum."

It was quite likely, of course, that Aldington was blowing off the steam of his internal combustion because D.H.L. had earlier pictured Hilda and Richard (as Robert and Julia Cunningham) in his book *Aaron's Rod* (1922)—and possibly part of the explo-

---

*Biographers have told us that Hilda Doolittle, after a miscarriage, reportedly told Aldington that she was no longer interested in sex and that he should look for it elsewhere. This he did, first with Dorothy Yorke, then Brigit Patmore, then Patmore's daughter-in-law. Hilda Doolittle and Aldington were married in 1918, separated in 1919, then divorced in 1938.

sion was due to the rumor about Perdita. Yet it was true also (as we have seen in other of his books) that Aldington's relations with his friends could almost always be characterized as "all men are enemies." This is especially shown in his book *Stepping Heavenward* (1931), whose delineation of T.S. Eliot (as Jeremy Pratt Cibber) can be called a caustic caricature. In the love affairs and/or marriages between some of the literati of this period the exchange of mates/mistresses sometimes took on the air of a game of musical chairs—and this too may have been the cause for Aldington's explosion.

In the merry-go-round that this book exposed (and Aldington's characteristic inclinations propelled), there was disclosed some literary history that otherwise might never have been revealed. The circle was partly closed when Hilda Doolittle (in the characters of Rafe Ashton and Bella Carter), in her 1960 book *Bid Me to Love,* pictured her ex-husband and Dorothy Yorke, and delineated in detail the break-up of her marriage. (In this book she included a picture of Ezra Pound—in the character of Lett Barnes—to whom she was engaged at the time.) The circle was completely closed when her next, or second book, *Helen of Egypt,* came out in 1961. In it she included the whole coterie of writers she had been associated with, in one way or another, during her life. In this book D.H.L. is Achilles, and the character of Paris is based on Aldington. It brought an end to the on-going-merry-go-round, for 1961 was also the year she died. It is the irony of fate that her books are almost forgotten, but that D.H.L.'s book *Aaron's Rod* and Aldington's *Death of a Hero,* the one published in 1922 and the other in 1929, are still being read.

Perhaps the only man to rival or exceed Aldington in his marital mazes was Ford Madox Hueffer (later Ford)—and, along with the amazing mazes of his marital woes, his absolutely unstinted use of people, mostly writers, in his books. Like D.H. Lawrence, Ford at times acted as though he was impishly motivated in his work because he, too, seemingly included everyone he knew in his books—sometimes so blatantly drawn in the *plein aire* method or so outrageously "like" their originals that he has been accused of wholesale reproductions. The fact that some of the pictures were published under the *nom de plume* of "Daniel Chaucer" was due, we know now, more to his unfortunate legal experiences with his first wife than from any embarrassment or effort to hide from whom he was writing about in his extensive use of acquaintances as models for his characters.

Ford began his romans à clef early in his career. In 1912, in his book *The New Humpty Dumpty*, it is possible to find that, besides the caricature of H.G. Wells (as we have seen), he also included a devastatingly destructive picture of his first wife, Elsie Martindale (in the character of Countess Macdonald), who wrote for the English *Review* that had been founded by Ford. When this marriage broke up, Ford married another writer, Violet Hunt, whom he included in his 1915 book *The Good Soldier*.

So far so good, but now the mazes turn into complex labyrinths and the images to blur—all to pester him the rest of his life—and all because of a book. Hueffer's legal and domestic complications began when his second wife, the poetess Violet Hunt, wrote a book and published it under the name of Mrs. Hueffer—which presumably would be entirely legal. However, the first Mrs. Hueffer (Elsie Martindale) pressed suit for libel on the ground that the second Mrs. Hueffer had no right to use the name "Mrs. Hueffer" because all the world would take it to mean the first Mrs. Hueffer. Strange as this action was, it is stranger yet that she won the case, and the book was not only withdrawn from publication and the unsold copies called back by the publisher, but damages were awarded. In addition she was awarded conjugal rights, and Hueffer was ordered by the court to live with her. This he refused to do and as a result he was jailed for contempt of court. One of the results of this *contretemps,* because of publicity surrounding it, was that Hueffer's artistic work suffered a startling reversal because no publisher would print his books. In order to overcome this handicap he used the pseudonym "Daniel Chaucer" for the books he wrote while imprisoned. After he was released from jail he changed his name and published his work as Ford Madox Ford.

Ford's life was so inextricably mixed with various women writers that, except for his work, it would be hard to decipher the who and where and when. His longest association was with the Australian painter Stella Bowen, with whom he lived for nine years. But, in 1931, while still living with Stella, Ford had an affair with the woman writer Jean Rhys, and he included a portrait of her, in the character of Lola Porter, in his 1931 novel *When the Wicked Men*. In turn, she pictured Ford, in the character of Hugh Heidler, in her book *Postures* that was later retitled *Quartet*. (A sidelight of this affair deserves a mention about these exchanges. When Rhys published *Postures* she also pictured in it her first husband, Jean Lenglet, as Stephan Zelli, and of course he in turn wrote about their marriage in his book *Barred*.)

From all of Ford's books—containing as they do the full-length portraits, pictures and/or sketches he made of his fellow-writers (men and women) it is possible to get much more than just a glimpse of the man himself: a knowledge also of his experiences, impressions, and nuances of an intellectual life seldom found in most novels of the era.* Yet there was change also. In his last book, *Henry For Hugh*, written in 1934, Ford modeled the main character, Henry Morton Smith, on the American writer Hart Crane who died in 1932. While not an important book, compared to some of his earlier ones, this was a switch from Ford's usual books about women.

In the matter of publishing family accounts in detail, Ford Madox Ford (who was always convinced that Henry James'

---

*The test: what one bit of intellectualism—or just a convincing bit of outstanding "intelligence"—can be found, for instance, in the Hemingway novels?

No Private Lives

character Martin Densher was modeled from him in James' book *The Wings of the Dove*) was not remiss in putting all his relations through the publishers' lists of his books. He put all the women in his life—Elsie Martindale, Violet Hunt, Stella Bowen (and who knows how many others?) in his books, sometimes more than once and under different names. Of the many, it is Violet Hunt who is "written down" in more volumes than any of the other loves.

In fact Violet Hunt appeared in so many books that a small library could be built around her "portraits," and conjecture hints that that is exactly what Ford Madox Ford tried to do. Not only was he the first to include her in his work, but the earliest was in his 1910 book *The Portrait*, in which she appeared as Lady Eshetford. In his 1911 book *Ladies Whose Bright Eyes*, he pictured her as Lady Dionissia de Egerton. In 1912 she appeared in his work *The New Humpty Dumpty* in the character of Lady Aldington. In 1913 she was the character of Augusta McPhail in Ford's *Mr. Fleight;* in 1915 she was pictured, in the character of Florence Dowell, in Ford's *The Good Soldier*. In 1923 he again pictured her (as Marie Elizabeth) in *The Marsden Case*. In 1924 she again "posed" (as Sylvia Tietjens) in Ford's four-volume *Parade's End*. From the number of appearances it would seem that this "affair" between Ford and Hunt was not only of long standing but of an equally strong affection, but Ford was one of the writers of this period who put many people in his work. In one of his 1913 books, *The Young Lovell,* he pictured his love affair with Brigit Patmore (as Clarissa Browning) when he was forty and already married. But Violet Hunt remains the queen of Ford's women insofar as being "pictured" is concerned. Because of the many times she appeared in Ford's books alone, it is a wonder of the literary world that she never pictured him in return.

As might be expected, Violet Hunt was "used" in books by other authors. Besides Ford, Arnold Bennett made use of her in his novel *Sacred and Profane Love*. H.G. Wells included her in his novel *Tono Bungay* (as Beatrice), and Somerset Maugham portrayed her (as Norah Nesbit) in *Of Human Bondage*. It was Maugham who first read Violet's book *Sooner or Later* that contained so many romans à clef that he termed it an autobiographical work. He was more prophetic than he knew, for in all of her work the reader can find character after character based on living writers . . . so much so that one biographer* said that she lived "more as a character in other writers' novels than as an author of her own." In addition to this penchant, Hunt wrote of her family perhaps more than any other writer, even Nancy Mitford. Instead of being content with one or two occasions of writing about herself and family, she did it in practically all her books.

It was no surprise, therefore, that even two years after her death in 1942 she appeared again in a book. This was Norah Hoult's novel *There Were No Windows* (1944), in which Violet appears for the last time (as Claire Temple), and where she is shown at her witty best and shoddy worst.

Perhaps Ford's woman-troubled life had its best years when he lived with Stella Bowen, although he put her into only two of his books. Stella, who lived with Ford for nine years, shared his life in both Paris and England, and bore him a daughter, appears (as Clarissa) in Ford's *Mr. Bosphorous and the Muses* (1923) and in his famous trilogy *Parade's End* (1924-1928) as Mrs. Valentine Wannop. But it was she who provided a fitting "closing chapter" in Ford's life. This occurred when Stella (who, twelve years after they had broken up in 1927, visited Ford on his deathbed at Honfleur, France) wrote her version of their life together in her book *Drawn From Life* (1940). Perhaps it was fitting, also, that a woman should have the last word about Ford.†

---

* Stanley Weintraub, but not a biographer of Violet Hunt.
†When Ford died in 1939 from uremia and heart failure, only three people attended his funeral—and a drunken grave-digger mistakenly buried him in

No Private Lives

H.G. Wells, in his novels, was almost as open in recording his love affairs as he was in living them. In his first work, *Tono Bungay*, he included his first wife, Isabel, and she appeared also in his work *The Days of the Comet*. His second wife, Amy Catherine Robbins (whom he called Jane), also was included in three of his books: in the novel *Meanwhile*, the second time in *Mr. Britling Sees It Through*, and as the character Ann Veronica Stuckly in his novel *Ann Veronica*. In the third book, while it may seem devoted solely to her, in fact it was not for it included also his first portrait of Rebecca West—who was to appear in several of Wells' works. Wells was adept in creating characters who were to appear in his work, and for West he created Miranda Morris who appears in *The Research Magnificent*, as Helen in *The World of William Clissold*, and as Martin Leeds in his work *The Secret Places of the Heart*, which was prophetic of the disenchantment and end of their love affair.

Following his break-up with West, Wells lived for eight years in the south of France with the Dutch magazine writer Odette Keun. This affair broke up with both writers annoyed with each other. She wrote a series of articles for *Time and Tide* magazine that debunked the world-famous writer and lover, and in turn he wrote another book—*Apropos Dolores*—that portrayed Odette as Dolores Wilbeck, and the picture left so little to the imagination that he had a hard time finding a publisher for the work. Wells also had an affair with the novelist Dorothy Richardson, who wrote about it (calling him Hypo Wilson) in her series of books, twelve volumes under one title, *Pilgrimage*.

Some innocuous "versions" of roman à clef (masquerading as

---

the wrong plot, so that the body had to be removed. It was an ignominious ending for one who had given so much life to the world of letters. It was similar to the burial fiasco of the French dramatist Henri Beque and has echoes in the unknown whereabouts of the ashes of Dorothy Parker before they were found (1987) on the mantlepiece of an office in downtown New York City twenty years after her cremation.

"history") have often occurred, such as showed Robert Graves and Siegfried Sassoon. Graves was limned (as David Cromlech) in Sassoon's *Memoirs of an Infantry Officer* (1930), and in the same year Graves portrayed Sassoon in his book *But It Still Goes On*. (Both books were innocent accounts of their shared war-time experiences, and did not venture any critical assessments or appraisals.)

But it was at this time, too, that Graves fell a victim of an occurrence so shaking that it was a miracle he was able to keep an equable balance. It was an occurrence where he was used in one of the strangest examples of novel writing ever to appear. This was the novel *A-14* (1930), written by Laura Riding (Graves' sometime wife) in collaboration with George Ellidye. It turned out to be one of literature's most outrageous examples of derogatory writing of roman à clef, so closely based as it was on Graves himself (the husband) and his family. In the book, he appears as Eric, his sister Rosaleen as Molly, his sister Norah McGuinèss as Maureen, and Graves' first wife Nancy Nicolson as Edith. Besides these there were many other real-life writers, including of course Laura Riding herself (as Catherine Phibbs). Critical reports on the book claimed it to be dull and tedious, and it made no particular stir outside the immediate Graves family and some friends. What was unmistakably disclosed in the book, however, was that Laura Riding—Graves' on-again, off-again serial wife—evidently mistook her eccentricities for genius. (Like Gertrude Stein before her.) In the biography of his father (1990), Richard Percival Graves reveals the poet's feelings about putting living people in books, and is explicit about the dangers of this practice: "writing about people without their permission is usually done as a frank act of hostility or disrespect." It was a *sotto voce* reiteration of the beliefs of Norman Douglas and a host of other writers.

As already seen, the majority of the cases that exhibited husband and wife scribbling about each other took place in the 'twenties and 'thirties, but even as early as 1913 John Galsworthy recorded the fading aspects of his marriage and depicted his wife, as Sylvia Doone, in his novel *The Dark Flower,* and a year later Leonard Woolf, the husband of Virginia Woolf, included her and her sister Vanessa Bell in his novel *The Wise Virgins*—to which Vanessa took exception, and she criticized him for using his friends for characters. This may be the reason he did not write another novel. Starting earlier, but continuing through this period also, was the affair between novelist Rose Macaulay and fellow novelist Gerald O'Donovan. In her 1918 book *What Not,* she depicted their relationship (he as the character Nicholas Chester) that started in 1918, when both were editors of publications, and continued until his death in 1942.

But almost as though it were a popular pastime, authors continued to put their spouses, *in toto,* into their books. Nancy Mitford, in her book *The Pursuit of Love,* painted her husband in dark hues, while Dorothy Richardson, in her 1948 novel *March Moonlight,* made light of her husband-writer Alan Odle in the character of Mr. Noble. Even a three-way round-robin of affairs-and-books took place when John Le Carré published his novel *The Naïve and Sentimental Lover* in 1971 that detailed his affair with Susan Kennaway (the character Helen in his book), who was the wife of Dr. James Kennaway who, it seems, set-up the triangular affair and wrote his book, *Some Gorgeous Accident,* based on it. And then Susan told her side of the story in her book *The Kennaway Papers.* The round-robin ended when Le Carré found it impossible to leave his wife and children and escape with Susan.

Some of the husband/wife scribbling—out of the ordinary as it was—had a humorous aspect or presented a sidelight that made it unusual and so brought it more to the public eye. Such was the case with Anthony Powell, author of a string of novels encompassed in his *A Dance to the Music of Time,* which is a continuing book of events sequenced in time (1951-1975). When he was once asked about the character of Isobel Tolland, he said: "a faint nuance (of which I am myself probably unaware) may to some extent mark her out as my wife. . . ." His wife was the biographer Violet Powell. Some of the "portraits" have been favorable. Aldous Huxley pictured his wife Maria in the character of Mrs. Quarles in his *Point Counterpoint.* Henry Williamson, in his book *The Pathway,* included his wife (who had borne six of his seven children) as Mary Ogilvie, and his book denoted only that he continued, after their divorce, to hold her in the highest esteem. Keeping him company was George Orwell who put his wife, Sonia Brownell, in the character of Julia in his satiric novel *1984* (1948). Hers is a pleasant picture among the grotesque caricatures that the author drew in the remainder of his book.

Not so fortunate was Evelyn Waugh, who earlier (in 1934) wrote a book, *A Handful of Dust,* that mirrored the break-up of his two-year marriage by picturing his ex-wife, Evelyn Gardner, in the character of Brenda Last.

That these affairs of spouses warring with each other in books are not just a modern peril besetting the rosy path of domestic bliss in the twentieth century can be seen in the similar occurrences of many years ago and in many lands.

The continental writers also had trouble with their spouses, or at least exposed their differences in print, as is easily seen in the books of many famous authors. As early as Dostoyevsky, one can see the practice put to use as he pictured his first wife, Maria, in the novel *The Insulted and the Injured.* Today all the world knows that Tolstoy not only included himself but his parents in *War and Peace,* and drew a portrait of his wife in *Anna Karenina.*

An outstanding case is that of August Strindberg, one of Sweden's famous and internationally known writers. Today it is believed that possibly the poverty of his early days was the direct cause of much of his cynicism, which of course later brought him unhappiness. Although married three times, he seemingly had a fanatical hatred of women. While he often wrote parts in his plays for his various wives, and they often played the portraiture of themselves on the stage, in too many cases it was apparent that they did not enjoy being dissected, poked fun at, and derided in his works. His marriages were even more tragic than his plays—to himself as well as the women involved—because he did not attempt to keep his opinions about them to himself, and out of his books and plays.

Strindberg was not the only author with this problem. In Italy, Gabrielle d'Annunzio, often called the father of Italian literary realism, in at least one instance went too far when he wrote the intimate details of his sex and love life with Eleonora Duse, using his novel *The Flame of Life* to show the ending of his love for her. Duse was shocked at the maestro's realism that consisted of calling her an old woman for whom his love was gone because her breasts had started to droop when she was forty-two.

Some French writers fared equally poorly. The author of *Gigi,* Sidonie-Gabrielle Colette, in her book *La Vagabond,* portrayed her first husband Henri Gautier-Villers who was also a novelist. Georges Simenon, in *Three Beds in Manhattan* (1946), pictured his second wife Denise in the character of Kay. Married in 1950 but divorced in 1960, when the marriage broke up, both writers shot shafts of recrimination against the other in their books.

It was more or less expected, when Simone de Beauvoir wrote her novel *The Mandarins,* that it would include a picture of Jean-Paul Sartre, her lover for over fifty years, in their "open" arrangement. What was not expected was the picture of Nelson Algren in the same book, in the character of Louis Brogan. He complained: "I've been in whorehouses all over the world, and the woman always closes the door. But this woman flung the door wide open and called in the public and the press." Algren also complained that while in *The Mandarins* he got the disguise of "Brogan," in another book Simone tried to make their affair appear to be a great international literary event.

While some of the books that have revealed the intimate love-life of husband/wife/lover have had a sardonic humor as well as devastating exposition, only a few have displayed any kind of poetic justice. The world's most outstanding example of this occurred when the German poet Heinrich Heine, whose marital existence was far from blissful, devised for his wife a written epistle that was at once the most devastating opinion of all time and also the epitome of poetic justice. The epistle was his will—wherein he left his spouse all his property and possessions on the condition that she remarry immediately upon his death. His will also contained the explanation: "because then there will be at least one man to regret my death."

In contrast to this were the picture(s) produced by Louis Aragon (who was himself depicted as Cyrille Galant in Pierre Drieu La Rochelles' book *Gilla* in 1939) of a single character, always a woman named "Elsa," who appeared, even in the titles, in four different books. This Elsa was patterned after Elsa Triolet, the Russian-born novelist who became Aragon's companion in 1928. His first use of her was in a 1942 book, then she appeared again in his books of 1959, 1963, and 1964. Supposedly this happened because he was inordinately fond of her, and their affair, even though publicized in the books he wrote, was merely his way of showing unchanging affection—and at the same time unmistakably was the opposite of the majority of such affairs.

And when the French author Marcel Jouhandeau published his work *Chroniques Maritales*—about the stormy life with his wife (the critics said it had been "written with an honesty that surpasses embarrassment and a wit so dry it burns")—the author made a terrifying legend of his wife as a monster. All of France awaited her book about Marcel, expecting it to be as destructive of him as his was of her. Instead, she simply stated: "Everyone has a cross to bear, and I thank God for Marcel Jouhandeau, who is my cross. But what a heavy cross!"

This was a mild reaction in comparison to what had happened when another French writer put a woman in a book. When Gustave Flaubert's mistress Louise Colet (whom he often neglected or ignored) first read *Madame Bovary* she became furiously angry with the author, thinking that the character "Emma" was drawn from her. She was amazed and shocked, and let the author know it in no uncertain terms, at what she thought was the novelist's double use of her. Flaubert had infrequent trysts with Colet, but he termed her his muse. The affair's seven-year existence was often turbulent and consisted of on-again, off-again arrangements. It was the usual relationship of an obscure writer with a famous, intellectual woman, one who was a much sought-after beauty. Although eleven years older, she was a woman who four times had won the poetry prize of the Académie Française—the only woman in French history to obtain such honor. That it was an on-again, off-again affair was due to the fact that they met only three or four times a year; their meeting, a day devoted to love-making in Paris at Colet's rooms at 21 Rue de Sevres. Occasionally they met at the Hôtel du Grand Cerf in Nantes, halfway between Flaubert's home at Rouen and Paris. Louise Colet was a highly sexed beauty who never hesitated to express her opinions. The affair lasted until 1854, by which time each had tired of the other's tirades and reprimands, and the on-and-off coupling. He (born December 12, 1821) was thirty-three and she forty-four. Except for the guessing games that many of the names of his characters evoke, only the real name of Madame Bovary and her husband are known for a certainty: Delphione and Dr. Eugene Delamare—and possibly (as only she would know) Louise Colet, who also contributed to the creation of a tragic heroine.

But Colet had ample reason to feel "used" as a model for

Madame Bovary. At the time of the book's appearance the common gossip of literary Paris was that anyone who knew Colet could not help but be aware of her when reading the book, since it "dripped with her essences." Colet's own written opinion of the work was that "it gave the impression of having been written by a traveling salesman"—perhaps in itself a reason for feeling "used."

But there were more concrete reasons as well. Colet knew for a certainty that Flaubert's description of Emma Bovary's romantic girlhood dreams came from her, since they were the same as her own, which she had disclosed to him. Then there was the cab ride where Emma surrenders to her lover—like the cab ride Colet and Flaubert had taken through the Bois de Boulogne in the early days of their affair. And there was the jeweled and inscribed cigar lighter she had given him, only now it was Emma giving it to her lover.

Although Colet wrote two books in revenge for *Madame Bovary,* only one is well known: *Lui,* in which Flaubert and Alfred de Musset play an important part since the authoress had been the mistress of both men. It was a book that Flaubert said he laughed over till he split his sides: "This is what it is to have copulated with the Muse," he said, using his pet name for Colet, evidently without perception that the book contained devastating references showing his miserliness, his insensitivity, and his gloomy periods of withdrawal. And he missed completely the definitive but unflattering portrait of himself that Colet drew in the character Léonce—a perfect revenge for *Madame Bovary.*

IX
The Quicksand Road

As happens many times in this world—when the flooding of an area (and why not an era, too?) has ended and the dampness seeped away—the roadway it once covered remains a dangerous sinkhole or quagmire that is difficult if not impossible for the traveler to traverse. Thus it has also been for our writers who unquestioningly followed the previously clear road to publication, success, fame or notoriety, and fortune, all by the simple expedient of putting real people in their books. Today, however, there are some potholes on this road—if indeed a road any longer exists—and where some semblances of it do remain, today's literature shows that it is somehow not really the same road as before. Very sadly it has changed into a quicksand road leading only to lawsuits, charges of libel, defamation of character, or even mental distress, monetary or character loss, and a host of other charges that can ruin a writer using the old method of including real or recognizable people for his book or story characters. Today the use of the old method is almost a sure-fire way of achieving the distinction of being sued—by friend as well as foe. (In one case it even involved an innocent inquirer.) Just how hazardous an undertaking this can be is seen from what happened to some writers in the recent past. For the writer there can be—besides the costs of a lawsuit won or lost—

the possibility of a book withdrawn from distribution or publication; there is also the possibility of a loss of an award or reward from an organization looking to bestow an honor on an author for work well done. These, in themselves, can be extremely expensive costs.

In the section on husbands and wives depicting each other in books there are, in addition, some occurrences that have an effect greater than mere ridicule or caricature. Such was the case when Louis Untermeyer, the poet whose troubles with his wife, Jean Starr Untermeyer, were for a time front-page news in many leading New York papers, suffered financially as well as in public esteem even though it was not he who publicized his marital woes. (This was different from the usual case, where it is the writers who generally do most of the reporting on their own woes.)

Again, in one of the world's most publicized family feuds because of a novel, we see Mary Lewisohn, the wife of the writer Ludwig Lewisohn, suing her ex-husband for $200,000 in a libel suit merely because he had written in one of his books "a woman can get a legal and social hold on a man that can utterly wreck his life." It has been reported that the ex-wife lived for more than fifteen years on the out-of-court settlement of the suit. If nothing else this case at least shows that a seemingly innocuous statement in a book can result in financial woe for the writer.

Other authors have also been sued for putting, or allegedly putting, real people in books. Among them, writers Betty Smith *(A Tree Grows In Brooklyn)*, Ilka Chase *(In Bed We Cry)*, and Marjorie Kinnan Rawlings *(Cross Creek)*. Betty Smith was sued for $250,000 by a cousin, Ilka Chase for $50,000 by a stranger, while Rawlings was sued for $100,000 by an acquaintance—all because the complainants thought they "saw" themselves in the books.

In 1944, one of the world's craziest lawsuits concerning a

writer took place when an indignant reader filed suit against author Arthur Train, accusing him of fraud in his "biography" of Ephraim Tutt, the main character of his book *Yankee Lawyer*, on the basis that the character Tutt could not be fictional but must be an actual person, or, if it was not an actual person, then must be a fraud because it was fiction. The complainant stated that he started the suit to make the author prove his contention that the series of stories about Tutt were not true but fiction. The author won his case when he pointed out that *Robinson Crusoe,* written by Daniel Defoe, was presented as an autobiography, and that Dean Swift's *Gulliver's Travels* was on the same order. A second action was then started by the same complainant on the grounds that Train's work was purported to be the work of Tutt, the fictional hero, while Train was actually the author. An injunction against the author was not allowed when the plaintiff asked for a rebate of from fifty cents to one dollar a book because of fraud. The second case, like the first, was settled when the court found no cause for action. But this—the world's only double-barrelled close-range shotgun blast at authordom by a single hunter, besides being a mixed-up attack on an author for representational (or misrepresentational) persons in a book—must remain at once the zenith and nadir of the dangers authors face when using the roman à clef method in books. Although thoroughly ridiculous, this case all too clearly resembled the heretofore amusing joke that had been around for a long time: that the author who is sued for putting a recognizable person in his work should in return seek an injunction against that person so he would not intrude himself in novels.

A more true-to-life plot involved Graham Greene. Although he wrote a book in 1934 entitled *It's a Battlefield* (about John Middleton Murry, although he did not know the other author), Greene could easily have used the title for one of his own experiences, one that should have warned him about writing too realistically. It began in 1979 when he was living in the south of

France, where he became involved in the legal affairs of a friend's daughter who had divorced her husband but was ordered by the court to continue living near her husband. Greene published a blast at the officials in a *J'accuse* article that charged them with corruption and claimed his life had been threatened. The government sued the author for his remarks, and after several years of court maneuvering, the author, in 1983, had to pay 30,000 francs in damages for libel.*

Even more recent occurrences disclose some additional dangers that today await any author who uses the roman à clef method of character drawing. Norah Ephron's book *Heartburn* depicted not only her husband (in real life Carl Bernstein, the Watergate reporter) but many Washington celebrities who were recognizable through the transparent disguises. While there was no trouble about the book, Bernstein nevertheless threatened legal action if the portrait of him in the movie version of the book was not toned down. From this, one can see that an author may be vulnerable not only because of the book he has written but also for its transposition to the screen—a danger not to be overlooked since so many books today end up with a movie or TV production.

The results of two very recent cases of libel and defamation auger repeatedly against the use of characters based on real people. One, the case of a lawsuit by a California therapist against novelist Gwen Davis, who pictured a therapist in her book conducting classes when all present were nude; and two, the lawsuit of Jane Anderson because of a movie company's portrayal of a character in Sylvia Plath's 1966 book *The Bell Jar* that supposedly implied a homosexual incident between two women some

---

*As may have been expected, Greene, as a result of this event, found himself, symbolically at least, in a book. Emma Tennant's work *Woman Beware Woman*, included a picture of a character for which Greene obviously was the prototype, the character of Hugo Pierce, a writer who tried to aid a woman in distress and was found dead.

The Quicksand Road

thirty-five years before, when both were mental patients. The Davis book was ruled against by the courts because it was held that the event depicted in the book could have pin-pointed the classroom strategy used by an actual therapist; the Anderson case of libel ended with an out-of-court settlement—even though it was acknowledged by both sides that the libelous implications could not be proved to be defaming. In other words—even if you do not libel or defame a person in your book, it is better to forego the use of any questionable "likeness," because you can be sued anyhow—and even if you didn't libel or defame the "likeness" you can lose the suit and pay damages. Another sad result, for the author, is that even if he "wins" the court case his defense can cost him more than the book might make.*

So damaging are the lawsuits for libel, defamation, and even the invasion of privacy, that today many publishers have a lawyer in their camp to look over every literary creation for potentially libelous material and to suggest revisions where it might be thought necessary—or what one man might think was necessary. This business of one man, or many, in an official position unrelated to publishing, making decisions on what or what is not publishable is the Tyranny of the New Age. It has a crippling effect on the creator, sinceit limits and restricts any use of material believed to be important but might be suspect. Of course this effects the expression of thought that may be desired to be made.

*As might be expected, there is an exception. When Frank Hardy published his book *Power Without Glory* he used the name "John West" which closely resembled the name of a real person. In making changes, the author neglected to change the name on all pages with the result that a lawsuit was started. What happened to the author and the book was the reverse of what usually happens in like cases. Hardy was somehow acquitted of all charges and the book allowed continued publication. Needless to say, the publicity accompanying the charges, the lawsuit, the trial, and the subsequent acquittal made the book an international best-seller. It was an unusual case, considering what has happened to most writers in like cases. It should not be taken as a model to follow.

All of which, of course, indicates rougher times ahead for our novelists in the future. It not only makes it harder for them to get a roman à clef even considered much less published—especially if one has not blunted the image to the point of nonrecognition, or on the other hand masked completely the perception one might ordinarily, as in the past, wanted to portray or divulge. This situation has already made a positive and extreme difference in the kind of novels we get today, when already we can see a surfeit of raunchy gothics, steamy sexuals, or horrid horrors usurping most of the space on bookstore shelves.

Of course, one method of avoiding such suits is to write only about the dead (since the dead cannot be libeled), or the novelist might decide to write only sweetness-and-light books that can automatically avoid suits but at the same time be far from what the author might want to say—perhaps even should say—in his book. It is a dilemma for any novelist whose work reflects his own life and experience, or anyone else's for that matter. It is possible to find the problem to be a human as well as an artistic one. Writers of fiction are notoriously easy targets for libel suits, it has been said, because their work is by its very nature untrue—and a false statement is one of the keys of what constitutes libel. The second key is that the work must in some way defame or expose the subject to contempt, ridicule, or hatred. Also, in fiction we have the anomaly where the First Amendment protection accorded journalists does not extend to novelists, basically because the libel is shown as fact and is not disclosed as opinion, which cannot be the subject of a libel suit. These are only some of the highlights of the dangers that can trip up a novelist, and are basically the reason why the roman à clef has passed the threshold to extinction, if it is not already extinct. For the new or young writer the message is clear since the dangers are real. Because he is writing close to home and has not yet learned to distance himself from his own life or experiences—and especially that of other peoples'—he can come a real cropper. From this situation it would seem that the writers who, in their work, would follow Philip Roth, Saul Bellow, John Updike, and others who made their career out of their own lives, loves, educational and home milieus, etc., will stop writing books like Roth's, Bellow's, and Updike's, particularly if their work includes anything "like" a living person.

For it can be a frightening—or at least a stultifying—experience for young or new writers who, to get their start, get known, get famous, get fortune, usually attempt to employ the "real" method. Since almost all first books are written from the personal viewpoint and experience of the author, it is only natural that the characters in his work mirror what he has seen, heard, felt, or known. And this, of course, can be fatal. There can be little doubt that this, along with the results of suits, which can be extremely costly whether won or not, is perhaps the major reason for the lowering of the previously high-flown flag of "freedom" and at the same time the extinguishing of the bright flame of "realism" that had lighted the way for many writers for more than half a century.

When George Keith Chesterton made his foolish remark, "The curious disappearance of satire from our literature is an instance of the fierce things fading from want of any principle to be fierce about," he showed that he did not know what the writers of his generation were doing, or that he was a poor observer and was better at writing detective novels than at commenting about the literature of his times. He was wrong, because the truth is that much of the novel writing from the first through the fourth decade (of the twentieth century) produced as much satire (and/or outright explosions of distemper, dislike, and denunciation) as any other era in literary history, in some instances even exceeding the best satire of the previous two centuries. A more recent and honest opinion is the one given by Tom Wolfe in his recent best-seller *The Bonfire of the Vanities:* "If you try to write about people of my world, the world of journalism and literature, the way people in journalism and literature write . . . about others, they shriek like wieners over an open fire—they can't stand it." It is true that there have been shrieks (as we have heard) from writers, but the majority of the ones who have rent the heavens with their noise are the younger, newer, or less experienced writers. (The shriek was seldom heard during the period when the progenitors were waxing at full strength—and then, if a loud shriek was heard, it was usually from a gun of like caliber exploding in retaliation. It was seldom if ever a matter of trying to get even or "scoring" by legal means.) And from these two viewpoints just given, it must be obvious to the most casual viewer that Wolfe's viewpoint is not only the more honest and correct opinion, but also the more truthful for two reasons: it especially fits today's writers as concerns their sensitivities, and it indicates that perhaps some roman à clef writing is still going on (perhaps *sotto voce*), or he would have heard no "shrieks."

Regardless of shrieks, or any other sound from the world's writers, the use of living people to populate our novels has been—as noted—going on for a long time; whether it will continue seems doubtful . . . and more doubtful as time goes on. This situation exists because of the advent of liabilities which the legal profession has inserted into the picture. Its demise began, it would seem, when we began to see on the front page of our novels the statement "any resemblance to actual persons or events is purely accidental and unintentional." The apparent need to include such a notice in a book is *prima facie* evidence that the legal beagles have already had a deadly effect upon our writers and drastically reduced—if not eradicated—all books faintly resembling a roman à clef or in any way indicating the possibility of a living person.

It has had an effect on our writers also, inevitably, inasmuch as writers write about people. If a writer's work is about himself it is less likely to be as interesting than if it is about other people, or a person known to many, for the simple reason that one person cannot hope to experience (and thus relate) the experience, feeling, or knowledge of all the things that "people" can—or a person who is already known for some peculiarity or idiosyncrasy. Perhaps part of the use of people—and especially writing people—can be laid at the door of George Bernard Shaw's statement to authors: "write what you know." Evidently many authors construed the advice to include "whom" you know, and their work reflects that there is nothing in the world that writers know better than other writers.

Wolfe's experience also tells us that the novels of this kind, in spite of the dangers, evidently are still being written, although probably much more discreetly than ever before. Whether this is for good or ill as concerns the value of the novels being produced today, at least the number seemingly has decreased, mostly because of the dangers attendant on the use of people-for-models method. Any decrease in the numbers, however, cannot help but attest that the stream of creative literature has been affected, with a good chance of being permanently dried-up. But one other thing that Wolfe tells us by his revelation is that it is the writers who are depicted in books that are doing the screaming—a much different result from what used to occur.

Although today we no longer have the spectacle of the literary dog eating or nibbling on its own tail (or cannibalizing the literary sect by publicizing the literati lives and loves, loosely or literally), something of its method still remains. It is the only explanation for the steady fusion of fiction, fact, fancy biography, and autobiography appearing in today's novels, all inextricably mixed so that it is impossible to tell where one begins and the other ends.

Let's face it. It has been claimed that one reason for this mixture is the difficulty, in modern life, of finding material for fiction that has not already been used a dozen times over, and as a result our authors have adopted the practice of putting their competitors under the spotlight. It was the excuse given fifty years ago; today it is even more valid.

But the question remains: why have so many of the world's famous authors depended on other authors for the material, or characters, in their books—or shown them, when used, in mostly unflattering poses? In addition to the reasons given there is one other: in this day of specialization ever getting more refined and explicit in all things (even fiction), realism has advanced so far that few care or even dare to write of anything or anyone that they do not know intimately—and our writers of novels have shown that there is nothing that they know so well as their brother writers. As Howard Lindsay, co-author of *Life With Father* (that depicted the Clarence Day family), has said: "Dog is an extremely tasty dish in a business where it's 'dog eat dog. . . .'"

But the day of such realism seemingly has come to a close. With the threat of lawsuits possible for several reasons, as well as an increase in nuisance suits by would-be collectors because they think they "see" themselves in certain roles, it is only natural that the novel of the past is no more, nor is it likely to be immediately resurrected. It is because of this situation that one frequently hears the original question: is our stream of creative literature drying up?

Of course, only time will tell—and, until the period that tells us the answer arrives, we can only review and compare what has gone before, and our benefits from it. A specific as well as a general evaluation is now due, perhaps overdue, of what we have seen, experienced, and known for the last one hundred years in literature.

At the least, the fifty-year deluge of a new realism in the world of letters that the roman à clef engendered, like the antediluvian flood of history, has given us a view of humanity and history that otherwise would probably have been slow to come, if ever. Its crowning glory, of course, is that almost all of these works (portraits of friend and foe alike), long after they were written, still provide us with a viewpoint and a message about oneself and literature that is unforgettable—because the work is unforgettable. If nothing else, the blossoming of the roman à clef for its own sake was something like a *Spring Awakening* and a *Götterdämmerung* all at one and the same time. Nothing like it had appeared in the world of letters since the Elizabethan age or the literary renaissance of the sixteenth century.

We would be remiss in our judgment if we did not admit, despite the present-day drawbacks and hindsight viewpoints on the correctness of roman à clef books, that this type of literature has provided the world with a scene and milieu of its protagonists that the world would not have known had the method not been used or expressed. In addition, since this has been a great part of both English and American modern literature, it has, to the extent that it has been used, enriched the world's literature—providing us with a body of work that consists not only of perfect examples of this type of work, or special school of writing, but are also outstanding works of art in themselves however they may be viewed. Besides giving us pictures of some characters and lives that were bordering on genius, by geniuses, they gave us also some views of ourselves that otherwise might never have been seen. From the twentieth-century writers alone who used the method, we find that we have gallery after gallery of artists who spiced their work, not only with unusual material and content, but favored it, and us, as a robust, vibrant life of an era with a type of literature that has few equals in the art of novel writing. In fact, they created for us a richly endowed art where we can find many artists who were specialists in excellent drawing techniques, others who were exemplary colorists, and some with a startling proclivity for getting absolute "likenesses." In all of this work, from the days of following in the footsteps of their progenitors, through the phases of being copy-cats and even mockingbirds, we have been given a rich heritage of a literature that equals if it does not exceed its forebears.

For one of its excellencies, of course, is that this "school" outshone its predecessors, giving rise to a group of portraitists to rank with the world's best. In providing this work that were perfect examples of this mode they also provided the world with a treasury of literary values, a literature rich in insightful, expository, and brilliant writing to the extent that they are not likely to be surpassed, or equaled—certainly not in the near future as the future of novel writing portends.

Perhaps there are some hidden ironies in all of this body of work which we have surveyed. While perhaps none of it can be classified as allegory, yet the allusions as well as the images with which it is crowded—in the majority of cases more apt to be real than not—provide us with a multi-faceted, many level gallery of pictures in a more than passing resemblance *à la sotie miroirs*.

For it is true that the work in this genre sometimes seems as if it had been done with mirrors, with each writer reflecting not only something of himself in each portrait, but in writing of his brothers has somehow achieved a painting in reverse also—something like the instant replay of football that is given from a different angle. Thus we find that most of the romans à clef resemble something of a one-way mirror that also gives a reflection a well as a clear view through the glass. In reality it is a "magic mirror" showing us not one, two, or perhaps more sides but many sides—and all at the same time. It was a method distinctive in itself.

Its passing from the scene of today will be a loss that the present as well as future generations may well mourn, for whatever takes its place will have a hard time trying to be a real counterpart to this past era's really "living" literature. As regards whatever in the future may take its place or exceed the past in its "realism" or performance in the printed page, one thing is certain: it has got to be better than "good"; it has to be exceedingly excellent even to share in the space and consideration earned by the progenitors, the copy-cats, and mockingbirds of the past.

Index

Acton, Harold, 35, 47
Adams, Franklin Pierce, 73
Adams, Henry Brooks, 91
Adams, John and Abigail, 91
Adams, Samuel Hopkins, 72
Addison, Joseph, 13
A.E. (George Russell), 21
Aiken, Conrad, 68, 75
Albee, Edward, 66
Aldington, Richard, 30, 40, 44, 100, 102, 103
Algren, Nelson, 63, 112
Anderson, Jane, 118
Anderson, Sherwood, 68n, 73, 79
Aragon, Louis, 112
Arlen, Michael, 30, 34, 39, 47
Arnold, Matthew, 20
Auchincloss, Louis, 84
Austin, Sir Alfred, 66

Bacheller, Irving, 67, 72
Bagnell, Enid, 35
Balzac, Honoré, 59, 61, 83
Bangs, John Kendrick, 67
Barres, Maurice, 62
Barrett, Edward Stannard, 15
Barrymores, The, 76
Barry, Philip, 76
Baughan, Edward A., 23
Beadwell, Maria, 11
Beaverbrook, Lord, 35, 111
Beerbohn, Max, 24

Behn, Alpha, 13
Behrman, S.N., 74, 75
Bell, Vanessa, 40, 109
Belloc, Hilaire, 56
Belloc-Lowndes, Marie, 56
Bellow, Saul, 68n, 83, 84, 121
Benét, Stephen Vincent, 77
Benét, William Rose, 68, 76, 92
Bennett, Arnold, 24, 34, 40, 42, 106
Benson, E.F., 20, 34
Bernhardt, Sarah, 61
Beque, Henri, 101n
Bernstein, Carl, 118
Berryman, John, 95
Besant, Walter, 20
Bierce, Ambrose, 68
Birmingham, G.A., 21
Bishop, John Peale, 78
Bjørnson, Bjørnstjerne, 63
Black, William, 72
Blessington, Lady Marguerite, 15n
Blunt, Wilfred, 17
Bodenheim, Maxwell, 68, 77
Bourget, Paul, 62
Boursalt, Edme, 58
Boyle, Kay, 30, 80n, 104, 105, 106
Bowen, Stella, 104, 105, 106
Brackett, Charles, 74
Brandes, George, 64
Breeding, Francis, 64
Brett, Dorothy, 30, 98
Brisbane, Arthur, 72

127

Britten, Lionell, 23
Brookes, Rupert, 34, 36
Brownell, Sonia, 110
Brush, Katherine, 77
Bullitt, Gerald, 46
Burgess, Anthony, 55
Burnett, Whit, 88
Burroughs, William and Joan, 87, 88, 89
Bury, Lady Charlotte, 15n
Butler, Samuel, 17
Bynner, Witter, 76, 99
Byron, Lord George Gordon, 14, 15, 76, 96

Caine, Hall, 21, 66
Caldwell, Erskine, 68n
Callaghan, Morley, 94
Campbell, Roy, 46
Camus, Albert, 65
Canaan, Gilbert, 23, 46, 97n
Canby, Henry Seidel, 42
Capote, Truman, 83
Carco, Francis, 62, 99n
Carr, John Dickson, 45
Carrel, Armand, 59
Cassady, Neal, 88, 89
Chapman, George, 13
Chase, Ilka, 116
Cheever, John, 33
Chesterton, G.K., 27, 45, 121
Churchill, Charles, 14
Churchill, Winston, 66, 69, 70
Clowes, Evelyn May, (see A. Riposte)
Cocteau, Jean, 62
Colby, Natalie Sedgwick, 92
Coleridge, Samuel Taylor, 14, 66
Colet, Louise, 61, 113, 114
Colette, Sidonie-Gabrielle, 62, 111
Columbier, Maria, 61
Colvin, Mrs. Sydney, 50
Congreve, William, 13
Conkling, Grace and Hilda, 68
Connolly, Cyril, 33, 35, 47
Constant, Benjamin, 60
Cook, George Cram, 73
Corelli, Marie, 66

Corke, Helen, 87
Corso, Gregory, 88, 89
Cournos, John, 30
Coward, Noel, 55, 74
Coxe, Howard, 53
Craigie, Pearl, 16
Crane, Hart, 105
Crawford, Oswald, 87
Crocker, John Wilson, 14n, 15, 17
Crosby, Harry and Caresse, 81n
Cumberland, Richard, 10, 122
Cunard, Nancy, 31, 39, 40
Cuppy, Will, 73

D'Annunzio, Gabrilele, 111
Dante, Gabriel, 12
Daudet, Alphonse, 62
Davenport, John, 33
Davis, Gwen, 118
Davis, Richard Harding, 67, 70
de Beauvoir, Simone, 63, 112, 113
de Castries, Marquise, 59
de Curial, Clementine, 60
Defoe, Daniel, 117
Dekker, Thomas, 12, 13
Delavanay, Emil, 99
de L'Isle-Adams, Verliers, 112
de Musset, Alfred, 60, 61
de Musset, Paul, 61
de Rochelles, Pierre, 112
DeVries, Peter, 83
Dickens, Charles, 11, 16, 17, 18
Dickenson, Emily, 73
Diderot, Denis, 58
Digby, Jane, 15, 15n, 59
Disraeli, Benjamin, 14, 15, 16, 17
Dodge, Mabel, (see Luhan)
Doolittle, Hilda, 24, 68, 97n, 100, 102
Dos Passos, John, 73, 80
Dostoyevsky, Fyodor, 63, 110
Douglas, Norman, 28, 29, 30, 32, 33, 45, 109
Dowson, Ernest, 34
Drabble, Margaret, 83
Dreiser, Theodore, 70
Drinkwater, John, 50

Index

Dryden, John, 13, 67
Du Maurier, George, 18, 19
Duncan, Robert, 89
Durrell, Lawrence, 42
Duse, Eleanore, 111

Eliot, Thomas S., 41, 42, 45, 68, 79
Ephron, Norah, 118
Ewing, Max, 73

Farr, Florence, 24, 96
Farrar, John Chapman, 77
Faulkner, William, 73, 95
Ferber, Edna, 73, 76
Feutwanger, Leon, 64
Fielding, Henry, 12, 13
Fitzgerald, F. Scott and Zelda, 73, 78, 93
Firbank, Ronald, 36
Flaubert, Gustave, 112, 113, 114
Fleming, Ian, 31n
Fletcher, John Gould, 68, 77
Ford, Ford Madox, 25, 26, 42, 45, 76, 80, 81, 82, 100, 103, 105, 106
Foote, Samuel, 13
Forster, E.M., 51
Forster, John, 11
France, Anatole, 61, 62
Frost, Robert, 68
Fuller, Henry Blake, 69
Fuller, Margaret, 65

Gale, Zona, 73
Gaddis, William, 88
Galsworthy, John, 47, 109
Gardner, Evelyn, 110
Garland, Hamlin, 69
Gauguin, Paul, 52
Gautier, Théophile, 59
Gautier-Villers, Henry, 11
Gay, John, 13
Gellhorn, Martha, 74, 95n
Gerhardt, William, 34, 47
Gibbs, Anthony, 34
Gibbs, Philip, 34
Gibbons, Floyd, 76

Gibbons, Stella, 56
Gilbert and Sullivan, 19
Gingrich, Arnold, 80
Ginsberg, Allen, 87, 88, 89
Gissing, George, 20, 27, 97
Glaspell, Susan, 73
Glenn, Isa, 76
Gogarty, Sir Oliver St. John, 35
Gogol, Nikoli, 63
Goldsmith, Oliver, 12
Gordon, Ruth, 76
Gosse, Edmund, 36, 43, 50
Gould, Donald, 42
Graham, Stephen, 42
Graves, Richard, 108
Graves, Robert, 42, 108
Greene, Graham, 31n, 117
Greene, Robert, 13
Gregg, Frances, 24
Grossmith, George, 20
Guttenbrunn, Roderick, 64

Hall, Marguerite Radclyffe, 34
Halper, Albert, 81
Hapgood, Hutchins, 71
Hardy, Frank, 119
Hardy, Thomas, 17, 50, 53, 77
Harris, Frank, 20
Hart-Davies, Rupert, 57
Hart, Moss, 74, 75
Harte, Bret, 68n
Hasting, Beatrice, 62
Hauptmann, Gerhard, 64
Hawthorne, Nathaniel, 65
Hearst, William Randolph, 72
Hecht, Ben and Rose, 77
Heine, Heinrich, 112
Helvetius, Charles-Adrien, 58
Hemingway, Ernest, 78, 80, 71, 782, 93, 94, 95
Henderson, Luanne, 88
Henry, Athur, 71
Herford, Oliver, 67
Hewlitt, Maurice, 15
Hichens, Robert, 20
Hinchman, Janet, 45
Hitler, Adolph, 64

Hobbes, John Oliver, 16
Hogarth, Kate and Mary, 11
Holmes, John Clellon, 87, 88
Hoult, Norah, 106
Howard, Geroge Bronson, 69
Howe, Irving, 84
Hoyt, Nancy, 76
Hueffer, Ford Madox, (*see* Ford Madox Ford)
Hume, Cyril, 77
Hunt, Leigh, 11, 76
Hunt, Violet, 27, 51, 97, 103, 105
Huxley, Aldous, 30, 31, 32, 38, 39, 42, 44, 47n, 120
Huxley, Thomas, 20

Juysman, Joris-Karl, 62

Ibsen, Henrick, 63
Isherwood, Christopher, 46

Jackson, Helen Hunt, 73
James, Henry, 18, 20, 24, 27, 51, 56, 66, 67, 105
James, Olive, 47
Jarrall, Randall, 89
Jeritza, Maria, 64
Johandreau, Marcel, 113
Johnson, Nunnally, 73
Johnson, Pamela Hansford, 43
Johnson, Dr. Samuel, 13, 14
Jonson, Ben, 12, 13
Joyce, James, 25, 26, 31n, 40, 41

Kaufman, George, 74, 75
Kavanagh, Paddy, 26
Keefe, Willard, 23
Kemp, Harry, 71, 73
Kennaway, James, 45, 109
Kennaway, Susan, 109
Kerouac, Jack, 85, 86, 87, 88, 89, 90
Keun, Odette, 27, 107, 108
Kingsley, Charles, 17
Kingsmill, Hugh, 34
Koestler, Arthur, 63
Kreymberg, Alfred, 68

Lamantia, Philip, 88
Lamartine, Alphonse, 59
Lamb, Lady Caroline, 14
Landor, Walter Savage, 1
Lane, Rose Wilder, 72, 81n
Langlet, Jean, 104
Lardner, Ring, 98
La Rochelle, Pierre Drieu, 112
Latimer, Margery, 73
Lascelles, Arnita, 23
Lawrence, D.H., 27, 28, 29, 30, 31, 38, 41, 43, 45, 91, 98, 99, 100, 102, 103
Lawrence, Frieda, 30, 31, 97, 98
Lawrence, Gertrude, 75
Lawrence, T.S., 42, 45
LeCarré, John, 45, 109
Levedan, Henri, 62
Lever, Charles, 16
Leverson, Ada, 55
Lewis, Grace Hegger, 92
Lewis, Sinclair, 76, 83, 92, 93
Lewis, Wyndham, 31, 32, 38, 41, 42, 43, 44, 45, 55
Lewisohn, Ludwig and Mary, 116
Lindsay, Howard, 124
Lindsay, Vachel, 68
Lippman, Walter, 84
Loeb, Harold, 80
Loomis, Charles Batell, 67
London, Jack, 68
Loos, Anita, 73
Lowell, Amy, 67
Lowell, James Russell, 67
Lowry, Malcolm, 73, 95
Lowry, Margerie Bonner, 73
Lucas, E.V., 17, 96
Ludwig, Emil, 64
Luhan, Mabel Dodge, 28, 30, 74, 98
Lyly, John, 13
Lytton, Lady Bulwer, 17, 96
Lytton, Lord Edward Bulwer, 17

Macaulay, Rose, 76, 109
Macaulay, Thomas Babington, 76
MacCarthy, Desmond, 35
Macdonnell, A.C., 35

Index

Mackenzie, Compton, 35, 57, 97n
McAlmon, Robert, 80
McCarthy, Mary, 83
McCloud, Daniel, 74
McClure, Michael, 88, 89
McCullock, Ferdinand, 43
McDonald, Dwight, 83
McLaw, Lafayette, 15
Magnus, Maurice, 28
Mailer, Norman, 68n, 83, 89
Mais, S.P.B., 47
Major, Charles, 67
Malamud, Bernard, 83
Mallock, William Hurrell, 20
Malraux, André, 63
Mann, Thomas, 64
Manning, Olive, 33
Mansfield, Katherine, 28, 31, 32, 62, 99, 99n
Markham, Edwin, 67, 69
Marston, John, 13
Martindale, Elsie, 103
Masters, Edgard Lee, 68, 92
Matthews, James Brander, 72
Maugham, William Somersset, 10, 31n, 38, 49, 51-57, 106
Mellows, James, 78
Mencken, Henry L., 73
Meredith, George, 17, 18, 36n, 50, 52
Meyers, Jeffrey, 39
Merrill, James, 89
Millay, Edna St. Vincent, 68, 83
Milne, A.A., 42
Milton, John, 10
Mitford, Nancy, 33, 109
Mizner, Wilson, 69
Modigliani, Amadeo, 62
Molière, Jean-Baptiste, 58, 59
Molnar, Ferenc, 64
Montesquieu, Robert, 62
Mordaunt, Elinor, (*see* A. Riposte)
Moore, Frankford, 15
Moore, George, 21, 70
Moore, Thomas, 15
Morrell, Lady Ottoline, 30
Morris, William, 21

Muggeridge, Malcolm, 46
Munday, Antony, 13
Murry, John Middleton, 31, 32, 42, 99, 117
Musset, Alfred de, 113
Musset, Paul de, 61
Mussolini, Benito, 64

Nathan, Geroge Jean, 78
Nash, Thomas, 13
Nichols, Robert, 43
Nicolson, Harold, 36, 46
Norris, Frank, 69
Norton, Lady Caroline, 13, 15

O'Brien, Mrs. Edward, 64
O'Brien, Flann, 26
Odle, Alan, 109
O'Donovan, Gerald, 109
O'Hara, John, 83
O'Neil, George, 74
O'Neill, Eugene, 73
Oppenheimer, George, 76
Orwell, George, 47, 110
Oulda, 57

Paget, Violet, 20, 66
Paine, Albert Bigelow, 72
Palissot, Charles, 58
Palmer, John, 64
Parker, Dorothy, 75, 76, 107
Parrish, Anne, 76
Pater, Walter, 20, 50
Patmore, Brigit, 101n, 105
Paterson, Isabel, 42, 73
Peacock, Thomas Love, 14, 18
Pegler, Westbrook, 77
Pfeiffer, Pauline, 94, 95n
Phillips, Stephen, 50
Pinero, Arthur Wing, 21
Planche, Gustave, 60
Plath, Sylvia, 83, 118
Pope, Alexander, 13, 38, 67
Porter, William Sydney (O. Henry), 69
Pound, Ezra, 24, 40, 41, 43, 44, 68, 79, 100, 102

Powell, Anthony, 34, 47, 110
Powell, Violet, 81, 110
Powys, John Cooper, 24
Priestley, J.B., 18, 42, 52
Proust, Marcel, 39, 50, 62
Pyne, Mary, 71

Rabelais, François, 59
Raphael, Frederick, 47
Rawlings, Marjorie Kinnan, 116
Reade, Charles, 70
Renan, Ernest, 62
Rexroth, Kenneth, 88
Rhys, Jean, 80, 104
Richard, Grant, 70
Richardson, Dorotny, 28, 108, 109
Richepin, Jean, 61
Richthoven, Baroness von, 100
Riding, Laura, 108
Riposte, A., 49, 53, 54
Rives, Hilda Erminie, 15
Roberts, Cecil, 34
Roberts, Morley, 20
Robertson, Tom, 21
Robbins, Catherine, 107
Robbins, Harold, 83
Robinson, Carolyn, 87, 88
Robinson, Edward Arlington, 68
Rochelles, Pierre Drieu, 112
Rodman, Maia, 82
Rose, Billy and Eleanor, 75
Rossetti, Dante Gabriel, 21
Rostand, Edmund, 62
Roth, Philip, 84, 120
Ruskin, John, 20, 50, 62
Russell, Bertrand, 30
Russell, George (A.E.), 21

Sand, Geroge, 10, 61
Sandburg, Carl, 68, 74
Sandeau, Jules, 60
Sartre, Jean-Paul, 63, 112
Sassoon, Siegfried, 42, 108
Saunders, Hilary, 64
Saunders, Lawrence, 77
Sayers, Dorothy, 45
Salinger, J.D., 69n

Schulberg, Budd, 78
Schwartz, Delmore, 84
Scollard, Clinton, 66
Scott, Sir Walter, 14
Second, Alberic, 59
Sedgwick, Natalie, (*see* Colby)
Shadwel, Thomas, 13
Shakespeare, William, 13
Shaw, George Bernard, 23, 24, 26, 87, 96, 97, 123
Shaw, Irwin, 82
Shelley, Mary, 15, 96
Shelley, Percy Bysshe, 14, 17, 96
Sheridan, Richard Brinsley, 10, 14
Simons, Roger, 83
Simenon, Georges, 111
Simpson, Eileen, 95
Sinclair, May, 34
Sitwell, Edith, 39, 42, 43, 44
Sitwell, Sir Osbert, 28, 39, 42, 43, 44
Sitwell, Sacheverell, 39, 42, 43
Smith, Betty, 116
Smith, Chad Powell, 79
Smith, Edward and Edith, 71
Smith, Stevie, 46
Smollett, Tobias, 13
Snow, G.P., 47
Snyder, Gary, 88, 89
Southey, Robert, 14
Spender, Stephen, 39
Spewack, Samuel and Bella, 75, 76
Squires, J.C., 35
Stanhope, Marianne, 15n
Stearns, Harold, 80, 81
Steele, Daniel, 12
Stein, Gertrude, 77, 82, 89, 94
Stephen, Sir Leslie, 18, 36
Sterling, George, 68
Sterne, Lawrence, 13
Stevens, Wallace, 68
Stevenson, Robert Louis, 18
Stewart, Donald Ogden, 80
Stoppard, Tom, 47
Strachey, Lytton, 36, 40, 51
Strindberg, Auguste, 111
Stringer, Arthur, 92
Susann, Jacqueline, 84

Index

Swinburne, Charles Algernon, 18
Swift, Dean, 67, 117
Symonds, J.A., 21

Tarkington, Booth, 67
Teasdale, Sara, 68
Tennant, Emma, 118n
Tennant, Margot, 34
Terry, Ellen, 72
Thackeray, William Makepeace, 16, 17
Theobold, 13
Thibault, Jacques Anatole, 61, 62
Thirkell, Angela, 46
Thomas, Dylan, 33, 83
Thompson, Dorothy, 92, 93
Thompson, Francis, 34
Thurber, James, 68n
Tolstoy, Leo, 110
Train, Arthur, 117
Triolet, Elsa, 112
Trollope, Anthony, 12, 17
Tunney, Gene, 23
Turgenev, Ivan, 63
Turner, W.J., 63
Twain, Mark, 67
Twysden, Duff, 80

Untermeyer, Louis and Jean Starr, 68, 116
Updike, John, 83, 121
Upland, Edward, 46

Vadja, Ernst, 63
Van Doren, Mark, 52
Van Druten, John, 76
Van Vechten, Carl, 73, 78
Verlaine, Paul, 61
Villon, François, 59
Voltaire, François Marie, 58
von Richtoven, Baroness, 100

Wagner, Richard, 64
Walkley, A.B., 23
Walpole, Horace, 13, 14
Walpole, Hugh, 42, 50-55
Walsh, Ernest, 80, 81n

Watts-Duntton, Theodore, 21
Ward, Mrs. Humphrey, 15, 20, 27, 32, 50, 60, 67
Waugh, Alec, 35, 40, 42, 44
Waugh, Evelyn, 31, 35, 41n, 51, 110
Webster, John, 13
Weekley, Ernest and Frieda, 30
Weintraub, Stanley, 106n
Wells, H.G., 25, 26, 27, 28, 47, 106, 107
Wells, Jane, 28
Welsh, Mary, 94, 95n
Went, Stanley, 52n
West, Anthony, 47, 48, 57
West, Rebecca, 27, 40, 47-48, 109
West, Victoria Sackville, 36, 46
Wharton, Edith, 66, 92
Whistler, James MacNeil, 18, 59
Wilcox, Ella Wheeler, 66
Wilde, Oscar, 18, 20, 36
Williams, Jean, 95
Williams, Tennessee, 95
Williamson, Henry, 24, 42, 47, 110
Wilson, Edmund, 73
Wilson, Roma, 64
Winchell, Walter, 75, 77
Wolfe, Thomas, 78, 83
Wolfe, Tom, 122, 123
Woolf, Leonard, 107
Woolf, Virginia, 23, 36, 39, 109
Woollcott, Alexander, 74, 75, 76
Wouk, Herman, 83
Wordsworth, William 14
Wylie, Elinor, 86, 92

Yates, Edmund, 17
Yeats, William Butler, 21, 24
Yorke, Dorothy, 101n, 102